M000318275

BEHIND THE MOUNTAIN

BEHIND THE MOUNTAIN

A Corporate Survival Book

Nick Williams

with Patricia Williams and Katie Thompson

DURBAN HOUSE PUBLISHING

Copyright © 2004, Nick Williams

All rights reserved. No part of this book may be used or reproduced in any
Manner whatsoever without the written permission of the Publisher.
Printed in Canada.
For information address:
Durban House Publishing Company, Inc.,
7502 Greenville Avenue, Suite 500, Dallas, Texas 75231

Library of Congress Cataloging-in-Publication Data
Williams, Nick, 1947-

Behind the Mountain / by Nick Williams

Library of Congress Catalog Card Number: 2003105045

p. cm.

ISBN 1-930754-37-X

First Edition

10 9 8 7 6 5 4 3 2 1

Visit our Web site at
http://www.durbanhouse.com

INTRODUCTION

Surviving for three days in sub-zero temperatures during a white-out changed my life.

During my career, I've learned about commitment, the importance of a positive attitude, resourcefulness, persistence and teamwork.

During the storm, these skills saved me.

I want my story to show you how.

Hopefully, you, the reader, will gain some insight into how these same qualities can help you in your day-to-day survival, in business and in life.

DEDICATION

To my wife, Patricia, for her partnership and love. And, to my children, Jennifer and Nicholas, for their love, understanding, and support throughout the years.

BEHIND THE MOUNTAIN

CHAPTER ONE

THE BEGINNING, THE END

Monday, Dec. 21
Morning

Nick

For the second night in a row I was leaning against a tree, face first, my back to the wind.

At 3:00 a.m., I awoke.

With the wind, it was 40 degrees below zero. It was December 21, the shortest day of the year. I could not stop shaking.

I kicked the rock face of the mountain with my ski boots, which were now blocks of ice. I did jumping jacks in the dark. I swung my arms. Nothing seemed to work.

My mind began to drift. I made a deal: "Give me my life and I will gladly give up my feet."

I checked my watch, over and over. It was a sturdy sports watch; it had been a Christmas gift from my children. I was determined to make it through one more night. I did more calisthenics.

I hoped for daybreak. I could not sleep, or I would die.

Patricia

The first batch of Christmas cookies was in the oven by 8:00 a.m.

Once again I had created what I hoped would be the perfect family holiday. It wasn't easy. Trying to get everyone together for Christmas in Florida took weeks. Our son Nicholas, a dental student, lived in New York City, while our daughter Jennifer, a lawyer, lived in Maryland. My 86-year-old father, also from Maryland, had already arrived. My husband, Nick, was squeezing in a quick ski trip before the holidays.

The tree was decorated. The Christmas shopping was done and all the presents were wrapped.

I was just waiting for my daughter and my husband to arrive.

I wondered why Nick hadn't called the night before. But after 28 years of marriage, I was used to these little separations.

I checked the clock again. Time to take out the cookies.

They were perfect.

CHAPTER TWO

THIS FAMILY, BEFORE

Nick Williams

I was living the good life.

In December 1998, I was 51 and CEO of Premisys Communications, a high-tech, high-flying company in Silicon Valley.

It was a long way from my hometown of Hubbard, Ohio. In Hubbard, I went to a Catholic high school; a priest there taught me to ski. I immediately took to the sport and over the years made time to ski, most often in Colorado. I became a good intermediate skier.

After high school, I attended the United States Naval Academy and upon graduation accepted a commission in the United States Marine Corps. While in the Marines, I was a Marine aviator and Avionics Divisions officer for a squadron of A-6 Intruders.

As part of my training, I attended jungle survival school. The first challenge was surviving in the wilds without being caught by "enemy soldiers"—Marine enlisted men dressed as Viet Cong.

3

We learned we could survive without food for several weeks, but without water for only several days.

The second challenge was another kind of survival: confinement in a simulated POW compound, complete with three-foot by five-foot wooden boxes as living quarters. During our stay we were subjected to conditions designed to break our spirit.

We learned how to survive—how to try to survive—in rough situations like these, with minimal food and water.

After the Marine Corps, I spent twenty-one years in another kind of survival school: the computer and telecommunications industries. I spent eight years with IBM, nine years with AT&T Paradyne, and four years with Tellabs Corporation. I survived in the business world, and thrived.

Throughout my career I always managed to stay in good physical condition. I was an avid runner and lifted weights on a regular basis.

Good thing.

Patricia Williams

I don't run a company; I run a family. From what everyone tells me, I do it very effectively.

Being a wife and a mother has been my life for the past thirty-one years. This has been a most satisfying and fulfilling life for me.

We grew up in the 1950s and my family was fairly affluent for those times. I didn't want for anything as a child. I like to say the only two things I ever remember asking for and not getting were a pony and a monkey.

I grew up in the kind of neighborhood where all of the kids were outside playing; that was my background.

Back in the '50s, I think everybody had the same family values. The respect for people, the hard work.

I had the same kind of background as Nick. I know I was fortunate. I got a wonderful college education. I was able to do just about everything I ever wanted to do.

I grew up outside of Baltimore in the suburbs. I went to parochial elementary and public high school.

When I graduated from high school, my parents built a home down on the Sever river, right outside of Annapolis. That became our home.

I went to the University of Maryland and got my degree in elementary education, then came back to the neighborhood as a student teacher at Sever Park Elementary. One of the other teachers was dating a midshipman in the 36th Company—Nick's company. She asked if I would like to go on a blind date. I didn't do blind dates. But I said, "Yeah, why not?"

The blind date was Nick.

I think it was love at first sight.

He was in his third year at the Naval Academy. He would come out in his uniform and approach my car and my heart would just flutter. I can bring that same feeling back right now if I think about it.

It was a wonderful romance.

We were married at the Naval Academy, under the swords. He was prepared to have a naval career, and I was prepared to be a military wife.

After we married, we moved to Pensacola for his flight training.

Then teaching became difficult. You had to guarantee the school board a full year, and military wives really can't do that because you never know when you're going to be picking up and packing and moving. I started tutoring for Navy Relief.

Then I got pregnant.

We agreed from day one I would stay home with our children. And that's what I did. I stayed home, I ran the house, I took care of the children, I took care of Nick, and it worked.

I volunteered. I spent years volunteering. I was the volunteer queen. Every school the kids went to, I volunteered my time, I tutored. I worked for the blind in Chicago; I was a docent. I wasn't a boring housewife who sat home and watched soap operas and ate bon-bons.

I'm not embarrassed to say I was a housewife. In fact, I'm proud to say I was a housewife. I loved it. I loved being able to stay home. I loved making a home for Nick and I loved making a home for our children.

I loved that life. Some of the best friends we have today are friends we made when we were in the military.

Jennifer Williams

I remember it being a wonderful childhood.

Both of our parents were always there, loving, helping us with homework. We were able to go on vacations. My mom stayed at home with us part-time, and worked part-time. Summertime was always playing in the pool and going to the beach. My dad traveled a lot, but they were both always there to help us with whatever we needed help with.

I always remember feeling safe, and loved. All the important things.

Joyce Canzionieri

We've all been friends for about 32 years.

They're as much a part of my life as anybody else. We've been together since the kids were babies, since before my youngest son and their son, Nickie, Jr., were born. It makes for a really close relationship.

Maryann Schoulz

Years ago, my husband and Nick worked for the same company.

We all met and just kind of clicked. Patricia and I got very close when we were all living in Florida. Then they moved to Chicago and we moved to New Jersey.

We're still best friends.

Teamwork:

Value of Good Relationships and Communication

My survival on the mountain depended on my team—even though the team didn't know the game was underway.

One excellent team player I have worked with is John Lattig, a senior salesman at IBM. John was in my sales team and covered several large insurance companies in the Washington, DC area.

He made 21 One Hundred Percent clubs and four Golden Circles while a salesman for 25 years. That's an amazing accomplishment. His customers always bought all of their equipment from IBM. He knew how to be a team player with IBMers and customers alike.

Whenever a large mainframe computer was being installed for one of his customers, John showed up in blue jeans to help pull cables with the IBM customer engineers and customer operations people. Usually, this occurred first thing in the morning, so John would be there with donuts and coffee—and an excellent attitude. He would help the technical people however he could. He was also present for the entire installation. If any difficulties came up, he could bring the right IBM resources in to fix them.

In our days as salespeople we did not have personal computers. We depended on "the word processing center"—a group of people with typewriters and other word processing equipment of the day.

Because of this dependence, preparing a proposal was a challenge. But John was a master at getting his proposals out on time. Why? He took the time to explain the importance of the proposal and the importance of the customer to the staff of the word processing center. When the proposal was complete and in the hands of the customer, John always followed up and let the word processing staff know the results. He bought gifts for the staff who helped him—usually a lunch to celebrate winning the proposal effort.

As a sales manager, I was given a trainee named François Maisonrouge, the son of an IBM executive. François was at IBM to learn some business skills on his way to Harvard for his MBA. I asked John Lattig to take him under his wing and teach him the ropes of what it takes to be a good IBM salesman.

John and François (whom John immediately nicknamed Frank "Redhouse," from the English translation of "Maisonrouge") devised a plan to sell IBM PCs to our entire customer base using IBM customer engineers— the guys who fixed the computers—as a source of intelligence on the competition.

The CEs, as we called them, spent a lot of time in the customers' computer rooms. They knew every piece of competitive gear coming in. As a result, John, François and the CEs sold a ton of PCs. I still remember a dinner celebration where John and François thanked the CEs for their help.

CHAPTER THREE

LET'S GO

Thursday, Dec. 17

Nick

For me the best part of living in San Francisco during my latest role—CEO of high-tech Premisys—was being close to the Sierra Nevada Mountains, and thus only three hours from the Lake Tahoe ski resorts. In a good year I could start skiing in early November, and keep going through April. It was common for the resorts to have a one-hundred-inch base by mid-January.

Life could not get much better.

Unfortunately, my wife, Patricia, did not share my passion for skiing. She loved the beach—the hotter the better. This worked out fine, however. On many occasions, I went to the slopes while she went to the beach.

Christmas 1998 was no different. On Thursday, Dec. 17th, she left our home in San Francisco for our second home in Clearwater Beach, Florida. I planned to meet the family there on the 22nd, and we would spend the Christmas holidays in Florida.

Meanwhile, I had time to ski.

I was excited because this was my first ski trip of the season. The resorts reported good snow and excellent conditions with ninety percent of the trails open. All I had to do was find a place to stay and someone to go with me.

Lodging was easy. I made reservations at a motel in Truckee for two rooms for Friday and Saturday and planned to have two days of fun on the slopes with my friends.

Finding friends to go along on such short notice was more difficult, but I'm not a CEO for nothing. I managed to talk my friend Roger into going with me; I also invited some friends visiting from Canada. They would all meet me at the resort.

It was going to be a great ski trip.

Claude Dupuis

I was in San Francisco from Ottawa with my wife. We were in the final process of deciding whether or not we were going to move to California.

Nick and I had dinner on Thursday night. The topic came up of whether we would go skiing.

We left it that I was going to talk it over with my wife, after dinner.

Patricia

During our marriage I think we moved about 13 times, between military and corporate life.

When we were young and got married, we thought we were just going to tackle the whole world. Nothing was too big.

For many, many years, that was exactly how we felt, and that's how we lived our life. Every problem that came around, we managed to get through it, solve it.

Some of the traits I learned as a military wife—you have to be so ready for when they pick up and pack out and leave—I was able to carry over to the corporate world. That's basically how it was there, too.

Every time you moved, you started over again. I learned to manage on my own because, a lot of the time, I was.

Linda McFarland

I was Nick's administrative assistant.

We had a holiday party on the Thursday before Christmas, the day before Nick went skiing. Nick was talking about who he was going to meet up there.

The weather report was not that bad at first. But it started getting worse. He said he was meeting Roger Dorf, and Claude and Paule Dupuis.

"Okay, well, you know, I just want to know where you're going," I said, "because you haven't left me an itinerary."

"Oh, don't worry about it," he said. "I'll only be skiing Saturday and Sunday."

Resourcefulness:

Be Prepared for Anything

When I was VP of Advanced Technology Products for Paradyne, part of my business unit was a wholly-owned subsidiary in Japan.

We signed a contract with a telecommunications company in Japan. The contract required modifications to our product to make it compatible with Japanese networks.

We made the modifications and expected to receive orders for the modified product. We didn't. We arranged a meeting between me and the director of operations for the Japanese company.

Before the meeting, we typed a letter outlining the terms of the contract, which we both had signed. It specifically stated how much product the Japanese company had committed to buy from us. We went to the meeting, intending to present the letter and state the key points to their director.

Our Japanese representative mentioned to me he should interpret for me during the meeting. He wanted to make sure that what was said was accurate.

He said if we used the other party's interpreter, our Japanese counterpart might not hear our requirements as precisely as we wished.

It worked. After the meeting, the Japanese company began to honor their commitments according to the contract.

CHAPTER FOUR

THE PLAN

Friday, Dec. 18

Claude Dupuis

My wife and I decided not to go skiing. My son was going to be playing in an all-star hockey game back in Ottawa, so we basically decided to fly back to Ottawa. I would have told Nick Friday morning we had decided not to go.

He was going to meet one of his friends up there to go skiing anyway.

Roger Dorf

Nick and I originally talked about going up on Friday, but I couldn't get away because of business. Nick was supposed to go up on Friday with Claude and Paule.

But I knew the place he was staying.

Nick

First Claude called. They just couldn't make the ski trip with me.

Then Roger called. He wouldn't be able to join me until Saturday night. We would meet at the motel, go to dinner, and he would ski with me all day on Sunday.

Saturday I would be on my own, but that was fine. I decided to leave Friday afternoon.

Friday afternoon I loaded up my SUV and headed for the slopes. It was a beautiful sunny day in San Francisco. I drove with the windows down and enjoyed the cool, crisp breeze off the Pacific Ocean. The drive from the Bay Area to Sacramento was uneventful. Traffic was fine.

The road from Sacramento to Truckee, where I had reservations, was a steady uphill climb. Along the way the temperature decreased and I could see more and more snow on the ground. I was exhilarated and ready for some good skiing.

I arrived at the motel and checked the current ski reports. Most of the resorts were reporting a 60-inch base and predicting light snow and warm temperatures for Saturday.

As I was checking in, the desk clerk asked for my license plate number. I went back out to the car and double-checked the plate. I had never done that before; I don't know why I did it then.

Commitment:

Making a Plan Work, Regardless

Some people can just make things happen, no matter what gets in their way.

I first worked with Roger Dorf at AT&T Paradyne. Roger was Executive VP and Chief Operating Officer. I was VP of North American Sales and then Vice President and General Manager of Advanced Technology Products Division.

Part of Roger's responsibility was global sales. He and his team in Asia worked very hard to get a meeting with the Director of Telecommunications for one of the big companies in China. After much positioning, the meeting was finally set.

"It was the Bank of China," says Roger, "in mainland China, back in the early 1990s. We went in to visit a customer. We were working on a bigger contract with them, and had three or four of their top people there, plus a couple of our managers and myself."

The team back home had prepared Roger for the trip. They briefed him on the customs and culture of business people in China. Since the person Roger was meeting was considered a dignitary, the meeting was arranged according to Chinese customs.

It would start with a business meeting in the afternoon to discuss the potential of working together and the use of AT&T Paradyne's products in the telephone network. Next would be a dinner for some socializing and more business discussions.

The most important part of the agenda would be dinner.

"They took us out to dinner at one of the local places; I was the guest of honor," says Roger.

The customary business dinner is fish. The table would be set for ten: the Chinese dignitary, the visitor, and their staff members, with a specific seating arrangement. A large fish would be prepared and brought to the table, head and tail still attached.

"They had a rotating table in the middle with appetizers, including boiled chickens feet, which I managed to avoid, but the fish head and tail are typically the honors," says Roger.

As the guest of honor, Roger was served the fish head.

The next-best part—the tail—went to the Chinese dignitary.

"While I was talking with their top man, he was eating the tail and talking," says Roger. "The tail was flapping, sticking out of his mouth as he chewed and talked."

Roger worked hard to keep a straight face.

"It's all part of doing the job," says Roger. "You eat things you wouldn't eat otherwise—fish eyeballs, stuff like that—and show respect. It's all part of doing what it takes."

THE SNOW

Saturday, Dec. 19
Morning

Nick

I woke at the crack of dawn.

The weather reports projected light snow and temperatures in the 30s, and I only planned to be gone for the morning, so I dressed light: hat, gloves, light-weight ski pants and my Dallas Cowboys jacket.

For some reason, I left my cell phone behind. I usually carry it everywhere, to the point of being annoying—just ask Patricia. But today I was traveling light.

I left Truckee and drove down the valley past the slopes of several area resorts. On the spur of the moment, when I saw the entrance for Squaw Valley resort, I decided that would be my target for the morning. I would ski Squaw Valley, one of the premier resorts in the Sierra Nevada mountain range. They have terrain for everyone.

I had arrived early and could already imagine my new tracks in fresh snow on a beautiful sunlit slope. I paid cash for a ticket and studied the trail map as I waited for the first ski lift to open. I rode the large gondola to Granite Chief, a 9,050-foot peak with intermediate and expert trails. From the gondola I could see there were very few skiers out this early, other than the ski patrol and me.

As the gondola rose to the peak, the weather changed. Clouds were rolling in and the wind was picking up.

At the peak, I hopped off and started my first run of the year. What a day!

My first runs of the day were on intermediate trails. This got me warmed up and acquainted with the mountain.

They were all good runs. There is nothing like being the first to make tracks in new snow. The scenery was spectacular. The pine trees were covered with fresh snow and were distinct against the backdrop of the valley below.

It felt great to be alive and skiing on this wonderful day.

Roger

I finished up my work in San Francisco and went up to Tahoe on Saturday. I left Saturday morning sometime and got caught in a snowstorm on the way up. In fact, they started closing the highways from there to Reno, except for four-wheel drives. I had a four-wheel drive Jeep.

It was turning into a blizzard. There was probably a foot of fresh snow.

The whole area was shutting down.

Positive Attitude:

Accepting Change with Grace

At several of the companies where I worked, I was responsible for international activity.

One area where we saw opportunity was Brazil. At that time there were 150 million people in Brazil—but the telephone penetration rate was only about 10 percent. Businesses had to wait for months to get even basic data services. Simply connecting to the phone system in some areas was troublesome.

I worked with a company in Brazil, an hour's drive from Rio de Janeiro. The company entrance was a locked gate; the guards were armed with Uzis.

There were phones at the company location, but using them wasn't simple. The standard noise in the handset was a warble. To get a dial tone, you had to dial a series of numbers. Usually, you just got a warble again.

But with patience, and a half-hour or hour of trying, you might get a dial tone and then make your call.

At the company, staff members were assigned to dial constantly to get dial tones for the executives. If I needed to make a call, I would tell one of the staff and they would get to work. They would eventually alert me: "I have dial tone, you can make your call."

I worked in this target-rich environment for about a year, trying to build a joint venture between the Brazilian company and ours.

There were many obstacles. The Brazilians thought

their company was worth more than the value we placed on it.

However, the CEO of the Brazilian company always kept a positive attitude. Our teams slogged through many negotiating sessions. At the end of each session the CEO was always a professional, offering refreshments and dinner and always pushing forward with renewed enthusiasm.

It took nearly a year, but it looked like we had reached a deal. We reviewed it with the appropriate people in both companies, and with the Brazilian government. I moved to Brazil to complete the transaction and to set up the new company as COO. The current Brazilian CEO was to stay in place.

Two weeks later, the CEO called me into his office.

"Nick, I really have to find a way to get paid for my investment in the phone company deal," he said.

"What investment?" I said.

He had paid a "consultant" $3 million to help win a key contract—the phone company deal. It was the core of the new business plan.

Over the past year, we had briefed the CEO a number of times about the U.S. Foreign Corrupt Practices Act. In a nutshell, it's illegal for a U.S. company to pay funds to obtain a contract. As COO, if I knew of this type of activity, I could go to jail. I reminded the CEO about this.

He went to his cabinet, retrieved the "Consulting Contract," and tore it up in front of me.

I asked him if he still intended to pay the contract.

"I must pay the $3 million," he said, "or I and my family will be in jeopardy."

As the CEO of an American joint venture, he would also be subject to the Foreign Corrupt Practices Act. I reminded him of this.

I told him I didn't think the deal could proceed, but I would check with our lawyers to be sure.

We had many conversations over the next week, but in the end had to cancel the deal. Throughout, the CEO maintained his positive attitude and professionalism. We parted as friends.

Eventually the CEO sold his company to a Brazilian firm, and I developed other business relationships in Brazil.

We both came out with success.

CHAPTER SIX

AND THEN

Saturday, Dec. 19
Afternoon

Nick

How fast things can change.

While riding the chair lift up the mountain after my fourth run, I studied the trail map and decided to take a challenging route—a run rated "black diamond."

As I got off the lift, I realized the weatherman had made a mistake. The sky was ominous, and the temperature was dropping fast. A heavy snow started and visibility dropped.

I wished for my warmer ski gear.

I decided not to take the black diamond run. I had to find an easier and safer way down the mountain. The intermediate trails I took earlier were safer, but led nowhere.

Studying my map, I saw a shortcut through the trees to an intermediate trail that did go somewhere: a lodge.

I took the shortcut.

Patricia

I was baking, decorating, wrapping, getting everything set at our home in Florida.

Nickie—Nick, Jr.—had come in, and he was catching up with all his friends. I was busy doing last-minute details.

My dad was there, Nickie was there, I was waiting for Jen to call. I was waiting for Nick to make his entrance.

He was supposed to be back in San Francisco Sunday night.

Nick

I followed the shortcut through the trees for about 15 minutes.

Skiing was very difficult and tiring. The new snow was deep and beginning to drift. I stopped to take a rest, took some snow in my mouth, let it melt, and drank it.

I remembered hearing you should let the snow melt in your mouth before swallowing. Eating snow lowers your body temperature and can damage internal organs.

As I rested, I assessed my situation. I considered removing my skis and walking back to the beginning of the shortcut.

But the snow was waist-high. I decided to continue on the shortcut with my skis.

The snow kept falling at a very rapid pace. It was getting deeper all the time.

As I skied through the trees, I stopped often to rest and drink snow. Sometimes I would have to alter my course significantly to avoid obstacles, including large trees. I had to go slowly and carefully to maneuver around them. There were also sheer rock faces and steep terrain.

This became a constant battle.

Nick Williams, Jr.

I was living in New York then. I flew down and met my mother and grandfather at the apartment in Florida.

From what I had understood, my father was going skiing on his way east. He was going to stop and do a day of skiing, and then he was going to come down for Christmas.

Nick

I hit a dead end.

It was a sheer vertical drop overlooking a valley about 500 feet below. The snow still fell and showed no signs of letting up. I did not know what to do. I considered taking off my skis and trying to climb down into the valley. It would probably lead to civilization.

I was worried. What should I do? Should I take off my skis and try to walk out? Should I begin walking and carry my skis for later use?

I decided to keep my skis on, side-step back as far as I could, and then ski in another direction. I hoped to find a ski lift or a lodge, or any type of shelter.

I side-stepped back up the mountain to a fairly high point and began to ski again. I hoped this was the opposite direction from the cliff.

I reached another dead end: the base of a mountain.

Frustrated and afraid, I ditched my skis next to a tree. I pushed through the snow on foot, using my poles.

With each step, I sank into the snow.

Roger

I was late checking into the hotel in Tahoe on Saturday because of severe weather conditions. The roads were open only to four-wheel-drive vehicles or those with chains. Many cars had run off the road.

When I finally got to the hotel, I had to dig through the snow just to get into the parking lot. I got there around 2:00 or 3:00 in the afternoon.

They gave me a key to the room, and Nick wasn't there. I was surprised to find Nick's clothes and brief-case in the room, but no sign of Nick, not even a note.

But I wasn't worried. Since the roads were so bad, I assumed Nick was stranded in one of the other ski resorts.

I fully expected to see Nick sometime during the night or early morning hours.

The thought was, "He'll show up back at the room sometime." There were clothes in the room, some extra ski stuff he had brought up for me, and all that stuff.

But I didn't go out to ski—not in a blizzard! Absolutely a blizzard.

Nick

The snow never stopped falling. It was a white-out; I couldn't see three feet. I couldn't see the sun, so I couldn't tell directions.

I kept crossing back over my tracks. This was discouraging. But what choice did I have but to keep moving? Moving kept me warm. Dressed the way I was, stopping would only lower my body temperature. I could freeze to death. This was not an option. I made a commitment to keep trudging through the snow.

Eventually, I saw a stream. I followed this until about 2:00 p.m. I hoped the stream would keep me on course and lead me to safety.

It did not. I reached another dead end: a drop-off between two steep cliff faces covered with large rocks.

Now I realized I was trapped. I was on the back side of this mountain and had little hope of getting out until the snow stopped.

I made a plan to survive no matter what:

1. I would move continuously during the day to keep the warmth in my body.

2. I would continue to drink the snow as much as possible because I knew I could live for weeks without food—but not without water.

3. I would find the best shelter possible during the night, but not lay down in the snow because my thin clothing would let cold seep through and I might freeze to death.

4. I would never give up until I reached safety.

I prayed to God to give me the courage and strength to follow my plan and make it to safety. My thoughts were with my family. I could not imagine never seeing them again. Prayer renewed my determination.

I followed the stream back in the opposite direction, away from the dead end. The snow was up to my thighs. Walking continued to get more and more difficult. I was warm, except for my feet, which had poor circulation in my ski boots.

I thought about stopping to take off my boots and massage

my feet. But I would have had to sit in the snow, and would have gotten too cold.

I kept moving. I kept looking for a way out.

I hoped someone would realize I was missing and send help.

Commitment:

Make your Plan, and Plan to Stick With It

From the time I realized I was in trouble on the mountain, I made a commitment to myself and to my family: I would find a way to survive and make it through.

There were many tests of this commitment. Cliffs, barriers, struggles in even simple tasks—not unlike many situations we encounter in business or life.

Mike Birck, founder and CEO of Tellabs corporation, has had his share of struggles.

When I joined Tellabs in 1993, the company had just come off a good year. Revenues were over $200 million and the company was profitable.

But Mike had been faced with a very tough decision only two years earlier. Competitors were announcing new products in the area of "intelligent multiplexing." Tellabs had a product in this area, and had recently begun developing a second-generation product called Titan.

The future success of the company, Mike believed, rested on Titan.

But there were only enough resources to invest fully in either the multiplexer, or in the Titan. Mike made a commitment to complete development of the Titan.

During the next few years, many people second-guessed his decision—including Wall Street analysts, shareholders and employees. Mike stuck to his commitment.

"This dog will hunt," he said.

It did. Titan became the most successful product in its category and Tellabs grew to be a multi-billion dollar company.

CHAPTER SEVEN

DARKNESS

Saturday, Dec. 19
Night

Nick

It was getting dark, and I needed to find shelter. It was only 4:00 p.m. I took cover in some pine trees. The branches were heavy with snow and sagged close to the ground, blocking some of the wind.

I picked a tree in the center and leaned face-forward against it. Tired and sweaty from my day's struggle, I took off my gloves and put them inside my shirt against my skin so they could dry. I tucked my hands up under my armpits, and pulled the collar of my jacket up to cover my neck and face. I vowed to move slower the next day so I wouldn't be so wet and cold at nightfall.

As the night got darker, I began to pray and think of my family and friends. I renewed my commitment to find a way out of my predicament. After a while the hard work of the day began to catch up with me. I nodded off leaning against the tree. Each time I fell fully asleep, my body moved away from the tree. This woke me up. While awake, I drank snow, said prayers and did calisthenics.

In my prayers I asked God to give me the strength to make it through this ordeal. My thoughts were constantly on my wife and children and my friends. I thought about being in Florida and enjoying a hot turkey dinner, spending time with my daughter Jennifer, my son Nicholas and my wife Patricia. My mouth watered as I thought about the turkey and about having a grouper sandwich at Frenchies, a favorite restaurant of ours in Clearwater. I hoped Patricia would be angry because I had not called her for two nights. Maybe her anger would lead to worry and she would realize I was missing and try to find me.

I knew I had made a big mistake by not telling her my plans for Squaw Valley. I hadn't told anyone.

Periodically during the night, I heard jet airliners flying over my position. I wondered if there might be a way the next day to signal one of them.

Meanwhile, the snow continued, the wind whipped, and I was freezing cold. My teeth chattered uncontrollably and I no longer had feeling in my toes. I kicked the tree I was leaning against to get feeling back into my feet. It didn't work.

Roger

I waited around, and then I went out to dinner by myself.

It was miserable even getting out for dinner. I managed to get to a place that was maybe a mile away. A little steak place in Truckee. There was practically nobody there, because it was just miserable, miserable. Nobody was going anywhere. I had a quick meal and went back, expecting all the time to hear from him.

I came back to the room around 8:30 p.m. and he's still not

there. No call, no nothing, so I called the front desk to see if there's been any messages or anything and—nothing. I dozed off.

I woke up and it's 11:00 and—no Nick.

I woke up, it's 3:00 a.m. and—no Nick.

I was worried, but I didn't know what the hell to do. Who do I call?

Nick

During the night I kept checking my watch. At 2:00 a.m. I thought, "Surely, someone saw my car on the parking lot after hours, realized I was missing, and sent out search parties."

The rest of the night was uneventful. I woke up periodically, drank snow, and did calisthenics. I did jumping jacks to raise my body temperature, and swung my arms in large circles to keep my hands warm. I touched my toes to get blood to flow to my head, stretched my back muscles, and kept my hamstrings ready to trudge through the deep snow in the morning.

Perseverance:

Stick with Your Plan in Tough Times

No doubt, if I had given up on the mountain, I would have died.

If you think back, you can remember your own situations where "sticking to it" made the difference between success and failure.

I learned the importance of perseverance early in my military career.

When I joined my A-6 squadron as a 23-year-old lieutenant and bombardier navigator, I was appointed the squadron Avionics Division Officer. The ADO is the person responsible for 80 Marines whose specialties are electronics, avionics and computer systems.

The Division must keep the twelve aircraft in the squadron in a high state of "systems readiness." This is essential; the squadron must be able to accomplish its mission of close air support for the Marine infantry divisions.

When I became the ADO, our squadron ranked last in the aircraft group in terms of systems readiness. Any of you who know Marines know being last at anything is not in their nature.

The non-commissioned officers in the division were convinced all of the problems were the responsibility of others—the infamous "they"—outside our division.

In particular, the Marine Aircraft Group could not get adequate replacement parts in a timely manner.

I knew I was in for a long, hard battle to get the

avionics division into shape.

I also knew I had little or no knowledge of the intricacies of electronics, avionics, and computer systems!

My first move was to meet with each of the NCOs and Marines in the division to ask why they thought we were last in the group.

Next I set up a series of meetings with the top four NCOs in the division. One was a master gunnery sergeant who had been in the Marine Corps for thirty years.

The purpose of these meetings was to set goals and objectives for the division, and for me to ask for help in learning the systems more completely. My admission I did not know much about avionics surprised the four NCOs and my asking for their help gave me credibility in their eyes.

Each was also extremely embarrassed by their low standing in the group.

I told them it was now my responsibility to take the heat for the results of the division and that I was prepared to do that. I told them it was their responsibility to help me identify the key problems that—together—we could fix. I told them it was our responsibility to ensure we had aggressive, achievable objectives. We would communicate them regularly to our troops, measure results weekly, and link the results to each Marine's performance in the division.

We had many knock-down, drag-out meetings before we agreed to a mission, goals and objectives for our division. But once we did, and started measuring ourselves against them, we started to become successful.

In a year we were the top squadron in the group in aircraft systems readiness.

CHAPTER EIGHT

OLD LOGS

Sunday, Dec. 20
Morning

Nick

The next day I awoke with the sun.

My plan for the day had not changed. I was still determined to find a way back to safety. There was a mountain to my left and my goal was to climb it. Hopefully, on the other side I would find a ski lodge—or at the very least, a ski lift.

This seemed like a sound plan in spite of the steep slope I would have to climb. After everything I had experienced so far, this was not too daunting.

Since the snow was up to my mid-thigh, trekking up the mountain would be slow going. The snow hadn't stopped falling since it began the day before. It was still a white-out. There was no way to tell direction, and the sun was not visible.

I kept climbing anyway.

After a while, I decided to check on my feet. They seemed too cold. To check them, however, I would have to get out of the wind and snow. There were many trees and bushes covered with snow; my hope was to use one of these to create a makeshift shelter. I dug out some snow between the trees and laid pine branches on the ground. Thus shielded, I took off my left boot.

This was not easy. My foot was swollen. Removing the boot was painful. I massaged my foot, especially my toes—they were cold and numb. I was frightened to realize I might suffer physical damage from exposure.

Then I tried to get my boot back on. I tried several times, but I just could not get my foot back in my boot. I knew I couldn't continue with only one boot.

Finally, by standing up and forcing down with all my weight I was able to jam the boot back on.

I realized I had better not remove my right boot.

I also gave up the idea of making some kind of shelter on the ground. The cold had begun to seep into my body even during the time I was working on my foot. The small shelter also limited my movement and lowered my body temperature. My plan to keep moving, I decided, was the right way to survive.

Boots on, I started walking up the mountain again. Several times I crossed over my own tracks. When this occurred, I would attempt to re-orient myself and move on. I continually looked for man-made objects. I hoped I would find a ski lift, a lodge or a cabin.

Finally, it happened: I saw a cabin.

I headed straight for it, imagining myself gathering firewood, building a fire and… maybe even finding some food! I could survive in a cabin for a long time and wait out the blizzard. I would warm my feet and everything would be okay.

But then I got close enough for a better look.

My "cabin" was a group of dead trees.

I was filled with disappointment, but I kept moving, hoping

there would be some type of shelter somewhere on this mountain.

As I reached the top of the mountain, the snow let up briefly and I could finally see where I was headed.

It was not good. Before me was a very narrow, very steep valley with rock cliffs on both sides. I could go no farther in this direction. I had to turn around and go back down the mountain.

Going down was much easier than coming up. By following my old tracks it was easy to gain momentum. I had to be careful not to slip.

The bottom of the mountain opened into a fairly flat valley. As I began to follow the valley, the sun broke through for a few minutes. I stopped, "drank" some snow and realized how quiet and how beautiful it was. The trees were all covered with fresh snow. The sun made the trees glisten. The falling snow reflected the sun's light in the spectrum of the rainbow. I realized how lucky I was to be alive. I said a prayer and asked God to keep me alive.

I vowed to keep going and was more determined than ever to find a way out.

Roger

Sunday morning, I woke up at the hotel in Truckee. Still no Nick.

I started calling around to see if there was any report of accidents. I called the Truckee sheriff's department, the California Highway Patrol.

I was relieved when no accidents were reported.

I left a note and headed back. At this point, I had no reason to believe there was anything wrong. My assumption was he and his friends went to Reno, or they're stuck somewhere and can't get through.

I had to be back that day, Sunday night. It was terrible, terrible weather, and it wasn't getting any better. So I left. I said, "I'll leave a note and I'll head on back." So I went on back. When I got back, I continued calling. I got nothing—not as far as any accidents or anything.

Attitude:

Follow the Positive

It is easy to have your hopes crushed. The challenge is to stay optimistic, positive.

This is tough during tough times, but being able to hang on to a positive attitude during difficult situations is an attribute that sets successful people apart from others.

Throughout my time on the mountain, I maintained an upbeat, positive attitude. In fact, the experience changed my perspective on life. I no longer worry about small things. What are small things? Work, for one. I still work hard and am committed to doing my best, but I rarely bring any business issues home with me. I am elated to be alive and thank God every day for all he has given me.

In business, a positive attitude is extremely important. No one wants to be around a person with a negative attitude, or a person who always picks out the negative aspects of a situation.

Customers *especially* are influenced by the attitude of sales people. In fact, anyone from a company who comes in contact with customers has the ability to influence the customer's perception of the company they represent.

The effect can be good—or bad.

In this example, I won't name names. I was working as a regional sales manager. A receptionist came to work one day with a negative attitude and proceeded to share it with everyone she contacted.

I received a call from one of our key customers, complaining. He said he had been treated as if it were a bother to put through his call. The receptionist was removed from her position, but not before causing quite a bit of damage.

Not every day can be an extremely good day for everyone. But each of us can adjust our attitude before we start the day. Look in the mirror, pull yourself up, go out and be positive. No excuses, no pointing fingers at the elusive "they." It's up to each of us to make sure we have a positive attitude when dealing with others.

In the case of a receptionist or anyone answering a phone, you should make the person on the other end of the call *glad* they called. This applies to internal and external customers alike. You never know when the person on the other end of the line will be an important customer—the one who pays everyone's salary and keeps the lights on.

I'm always amazed when I interact with a negative sales person or any negative company representative. Do they know they may be destroying a customer relationship?

FAILURE

Sunday, Dec. 20
Afternoon

Nick

I kept trudging through the valley. The snow was up to my waist in some spots. The brief view of the sun had given me some sense of direction. I had renewed energy and I knew I was going to find a way out or be found today.

Then I fell.

While walking through an area of very deep snow, I felt myself falling straight down. To my horror, I had fallen into a stream bed hidden under the snow. The water in the stream bed was just deep enough to fill my boots. Now, my feet were not only cold and numb, but also wet.

This was a dangerous combination. Now I was certain my feet would suffer extreme frostbite. I thought about taking my boots off and pouring out the water. But after my earlier struggle with my left boot I knew I couldn't risk it. It would be a disaster if I couldn't put my boots back on.

I had no other choice but to keep moving. I stopped long enough to take advantage of the clear running stream and drank my fill.

It was December 20. I knew tomorrow, December 21, would be the shortest day of the year. This stuck in my mind as I was walking. I worried it would get dark early and knew warmth and shelter were important, especially for my feet.

Another thought kept running through my mind: Why aren't the rescuers out looking for me?

Certainly, someone knows I am missing by now. My car would have been found in the parking lot. Patricia and Roger must realize I am in trouble. Why haven't they sent out a rescue team?

As the terrain began to slope upward, I hoped I was heading in the right direction, back toward the ski lifts. There were large rocks in this part of the valley.

I found a flat granite rock face that was about twenty feet high and thirty feet wide. It was surrounded by trees and provided some protection from the wind. My plan was to build a fire and try to thaw my feet, which were now frozen.

I gathered kindling and stacked it at the base of the rock face. I had no matches, so I struck the granite rock face with the metal tip of my ski pole. Sparks began to flow onto the kindling wood. This was exciting! However, the wood did not ignite. I had some twenty dollar bills in my wallet and placed some on the kindling, hoping they would ignite. Eventually, the metal tip on my ski pole broke off on the granite.

I started again with my second ski pole. Still the wood and twenty dollar bills would not ignite. Finally, the tip broke off my second ski pole. I had failed to start a fire.

On a positive note, this activity kept most of my body warm for two hours. My feet were the exception. They were still frozen, now encased in blocks of ice in my boots.

Roger

Sunday afternoon, I still hadn't found any police reports of accidents.

There was one nagging thought: Why didn't Nick call? That was one thing nagging at me all this time. Surely—he'd call.

Back before I was married, I had an insurance guy in Minnesota when I was first working for IBM. He just all of a sudden disappeared. He's one of these major community guys—a family man, yada yada yada—and he just disappeared one day, and nobody knew where the hell he went. He turned up five or six years later. He had simply checked out. He had gone away to be a truck driver or something, and then just showed up again one day.

Another time, a brother of a dear friend of ours had gone out fishing in Lake Superior in a rowboat and the rowboat came back empty. They assumed he was dead—drowned. He showed up a few years later.

These were two things in the back of my mind. "So," I thought, "has Nick skipped out on life?" That was one possibility that ran through my mind. I said, "This is very strange." I'd had these two experiences where people had just disappeared. Very stable people. One a doctor, another an insurance salesman— strong family mean. So these are all the kind of things that run through your mind. "What's going on?"

Or "Did he have a girlfriend?"

Not the kind of guy I would *ever* have expected. I had known Nick for a long time, gone many places together with him, and he was one of the last people I would have expected was messing around, frankly.

Patricia

I figured he had probably gotten in late but didn't want to call because he knew my dad was here with us in Florida.

Let's say he got in late, at 11:00, after a full day of skiing. That would be two in the morning for us. That's why I didn't think anything of it.

The time change made everything difficult.

Resourcefulness:

Invent Tools and Use Them

Sometimes you just have to make do.

In today's business environment, resourcefulness is essential for success.

When I was hired at Paradyne, I had to make do. I was the new Regional Manager of Federal Sales. Unfortunately, we were in the midst of being suspended from making federal sales.

My boss asked me to find a way to continue selling our products even if we were suspended. I enlisted the help of the Federal Sales Manager, Jim Spain.

"Before Nick or I were at Paradyne," says Jim, "the company had a contract with the Social Security Administration."

However, the Social Security Administration got extra attention from some members of Congress—to this day Social Security is a political hot potato.

"Our contract came under scrutiny by one of these congressmen because somebody said we won the contract through smoke and mirrors," says Jim. By now, Jim and I were both at Paradyne.

"The congressman tried to suspend us from government operations, and we disagreed," says Jim. "Our chairman challenged him publicly, in the press. That was a political mistake."

But it happened. We got suspended. For more than a year, we could not do any new business with the federal government while we fought to prove our innocence.

How could we keep our federal business alive?

"We did three things," says Jim. "First, we learned the nuances of doing business with the federal government. What was legal, and what wasn't? What could we do, and what couldn't we do?"

The regulations fill two three-inch binders.

"Second," he says, "we met with the senior people in companies where we had contracts." We could keep doing business with them—if they believed in us. We tried very hard to make that happen, and it generally did.

In fact, we had been trying to meet with these same agency heads for years, but hadn't gotten in. Now, because of the suspension, this quirk in the rules got us in the door.

"Third," he says, "we put together an incentive plan that would let us keep paying our sales staff even though they weren't able to make new sales. We used MBOs—management by objectives—to measure their performance each quarter. If they were doing the right things, they would get paid as much as if they had been making sales. This ended up building relationships that led to quicker sales after the suspension ended."

The results of our plan were phenomenal. We retained every single contract, and after review of our performance, the agency higher-ups gave us their blessing and guidance on how to continue to do business with them.

Sales increased in our federal area during the time we were suspended.

Jim Spain is now the managing partner of Federal Sales Associates, a consulting company focusing on emerging technology companies looking to enter the federal sector.

CHAPTER TEN

ON YOUR KNEES

Sunday, Dec. 20
Night

Nick

Night fell. The wind whipped through the trees. With the wind, the temperature during the night dropped to 40 below zero.

I leaned against a tree, my face against the rough bark, for the second night in a row.

At around 3:00 a.m., I awoke. I could not stop myself from shivering. I could feel my body temperature getting lower and lower. I kicked the rock face to try to get some blood flowing into my feet, swung my arms in large circles, and did jumping jacks. Nothing seemed to work.

My mind began to drift and I began to wonder: "Is this how it is when you get close to death?" Praying and thinking of my family and friends once more, I made a deal with God:

"If you just give me my life I would gladly give up my feet."

I thought of people who have no legs and still get through

life. I remembered reading about courageous people who could still walk, run, and ski without the use of their legs. If they could continue to live a normal life without legs, I could certainly do it without feet. I was afraid to fall asleep because I thought I might freeze to death.

Determined to make it through one more night, I did more calisthenics and managed to stay awake. Hoping for daybreak, I continually looked at my watch.

Roger

I got back home pretty late because of the weather. I made a few calls and I got nothing.

There hadn't been any word from Nick, but I wasn't too worried.

Still, it bothered me. I left messages on Nick's home phone, cell phone and office phone.

Jim Ashby
National Weather Service

That weekend they got about nine inches of new snow at Tahoe City. You're obviously going to get a little bit more in the mountains. Truckee got 22 inches during that storm.

It was certainly colder than what you'd normally expect for any time of year. It was an *extremely* cold snap right around that time.

The 18th was pretty warm. That was before the cold air moved in.

Knowing what it's like around here, it was probably very windy when that cold air moved in. And up on top of the mountain? Definitely, oh absolutely.

Roger

I said to myself, "He's with Claude and Paule." I was upset I hadn't heard anything from him, but—he's not by himself.

But I'm still having trouble sleeping. I couldn't understand what was going on. There was something strange here.

I was home in San Francisco by myself. My wife, Sandy, was in Colorado. Patricia had been with her in Colorado before she went to Florida.

I talked with Sandy on Sunday. It's a rare day when one of us has gone away that we don't talk. I know we talked on Sunday.

I said, "This is very strange. But I don't think I want to call Patricia yet, because I don't know what's going on here. I don't want to alarm her."

But still. What the hell's going on here?

It was almost irritating, as if Nick was being thoughtless.

Why didn't he leave a note? Why didn't he tell me where he's going? Where are they?

Patricia

Sunday night I went to bed with visions of sugar plums in my head. The tree was decorated. All the Christmas shopping was done and all the presents were wrapped.

Once again I had created what I hoped would be the perfect family holiday. The logistics alone made this a challenge! Our son Nicholas was a dental student in New York City. Jennifer, our daughter, was practicing law for a firm in Columbia, Maryland. Trying to get everyone together for Christmas in Florida took weeks to orchestrate.

But I did it.

Now Nickie was home for the holidays. My father was visiting from Maryland. I was just waiting for Jennifer and my husband Nick to arrive.

Nick, Jr.

Dad was supposed to call, and he didn't call. So my mother got very worried. At first she wasn't as worried. But as time progressed and he still hadn't called, then we started to worry.

I didn't think he'd been skiing. Sometimes my father just does things he wants to do. I figured maybe he stopped somewhere else on the way, or maybe he just dropped his cell phone in the water… I didn't know what happened.

I thought he was being absent-minded. That's what I thought. I didn't think anything bad had come about.

Perseverance:

Never, Ever Quit

Sometimes, the person who wins is simply the one who didn't quit.

Ray Cheung worked with me at Tellabs Corporation. He had responsibility for the Asia Pacific region. He lived in Singapore while his wife, Mauricette, lived in London. Mauricette worked for British Airways and commuted to Singapore on some weekends so she and Ray could be together.

Ray had been working for British Telecom before he came to Tellabs. He had managed the Asia Pacific region and was very successful.

When he took over the region for Tellabs, we were in the process of losing our largest customer in Asia Pacific to a competitor. This competitor had been very successful throughout the international marketplace, especially in the Asia Pacific.

Our competitor had already received a letter of intent from our customer for their product line. It would replace ours.

Enter Ray Cheung.

Tellabs had just acquired Martis, a Finnish company. Their product line might—just might—be a good fit for the customer we were near losing.

Ray went right to the top of the customer's organization and met with their managing director. He took many trips to Finland and Lisle, Illinois—corporate HQ for

Tellabs. He browbeat the Finns to make adjustments to the Martis product so it could satisfy the customer's needs.

The result: We took away a $10 million order from the competitor, and our customer became a $50 million account over the next five years.

All thanks to the perseverance of Ray Cheung.

CHAPTER ELEVEN

REACHING OUT

Monday, Dec. 21
Morning

Nick

Early the next morning as the landscape started to brighten, I thanked God for helping me make it through the night. I resolved to get back to safety.

Finally, the snow had stopped and the rising sun helped me determine direction. The trail map indicated trails and lodges to the northeast, so I began moving just to the left of where I thought the sun would rise.

The climb was straight uphill and the wind was blowing directly in my face. I remember thinking: "Dear God, you are not going to make any of this easy, are you? I guess you are testing my resolve. Well, I *am* going to keep pushing through this snow and I *am* going to make it. Please help me."

The snow had drifted in many areas. At times, I pushed through drifts that were up to my chest or found a way around them. It depended on the slope of the hill and the strength of the wind at the time.

Always, I kept focused on where I thought the sun would rise and tried to keep moving in a north-easterly direction.

Although my feet were frozen and had lost all feeling, they did not hinder my progress.

Roger

I get up Monday morning and say, "This is really strange." The first thing I did was call Nick's office. I knew he was an early bird.

"Is Nick in?" I asked.

"No," said his assistant, Linda.

"Have you heard from him?"

"No. Did you ski with him this weekend?" she says.

"No," I said. "He didn't show. He was supposed to be with Claude and Paule."

And she says, "Well, let me call them. I think they went back to Canada."

So she called, and then called me back.

"They're in Canada," she says. "They're not with Nick."

That's when the cold chills went up the back of my neck. "Oh my god," I said.

So, we said, let's get to work. Now. We agreed to start calling, hospitals and such.

She had a list, and I had a list, and we started calling.

We thought there must have been an auto accident—that the guy can't talk, he's in a hospital somewhere.

"Lost" wasn't even a thought.

Not yet.

Patricia

I put the first batch of Christmas cookies in the oven by 8:00 a.m. Monday.

I wondered why Nick hadn't called the previous night. There was no doubt he would call—we needed to coordinate our last-minute plans for Christmas.

I was watching the clock. As soon as it was 8:30 a.m.—5:30 a.m. West coast time—I expected the phone to ring: Nick.

When it didn't, I called him. There was no answer at home, nor on his cell phone.

Still, I had no reason to worry. After twenty-eight years of marriage, I was used to these separations. Nick traveled frequently with his job, and over the years we had gotten lax about checking in with each other.

This is a pattern I don't recommend for couples.

Linda

Usually I get in about eight. When I came in that morning, Monday, it was about 8:15, and Nick's office was dark. My intuition was something was wrong.

I check voice mail and—nothing from Nick.

I check e-mail—nothing from Nick.

I call his cell—he doesn't pick up.

I call his home—nobody answers.

Now, that is not like Nick. He's always there at seven. Plus, he has a staff meeting at ten. It was totally unlike him to be out of touch.

I had a voice mail from Roger. He said, "Have Nick call me when he gets in."

I could have just waited, but my intuition said "this is SO unlike Nick". He's very predictable, very consistent.

Somebody would have let me know if he wasn't going to be there. But nobody did. That's why I took action right away. I knew it wasn't normal.

I called Roger.

"Roger—did you hook up with Nick?"

He goes, "You know, I didn't. What happened?"

He said, it's horrible weather. I finally got up there, he told me. I waited at the hotel. He had mentioned there were other friends, some of the roads were closed, I thought he was stuck somewhere. "So the next morning," he said, "I got up, Nick wasn't back, and I—went home."

I say, "What's the hotel number? Nick is nowhere. I don't know where to find him. And he has a meeting at ten."

He said, "It's okay—I'll call the hotel." He called the hotel.

He called me back. He says, "He never checked back in."

I said, "Oh, this is not good."

And it wasn't.

We started making phone calls. We didn't learn anything. We didn't find Nick. We needed more information.

"How do we get his car license number?" I said.

And then it was time.

He said, "I think I had better call Patricia."

And he did.

Teamwork:

Don't Be Afraid to Reach Out

Teamwork was going to be the key to finding me on the mountain. Teamwork is also extremely important in today's business environment.

Rarely are people successful in dealing with customers without calling on the entire company team to help out. Those who recognize this and treat team members with dignity and respect—and thank them for their efforts—are usually the most successful people in a company.

An example of this is something I learned while in Silicon Valley as CEO of Premisys. Another CEO in the Valley started a practice of inviting employees to attend a breakfast with him on the day of their birthday. I used this same technique at Premisys, and at other companies since then, to encourage communication and teamwork among employees and managers.

In another version of this, the "birthday meeting" is held monthly. Anyone whose birthday occurs in a given month is invited to attend a two-hour breakfast meeting with the CEO or other executive. Inviting people on their birthday month quite often results in a very cross-functional group attending the meeting.

The agenda of the meeting, published ahead of time, is as follows:

The employees are encouraged to ask any questions they have about the company—no holds barred.

They are then asked a question: What would you do

to improve the company if you were the CEO?

The ideas for improvement are written on sticky notes and placed on a wall or blackboard.

The ideas are then categorized and, via email, the employees are asked to vote on their top five. The votes are tabulated and the top two areas for improvement are brought to the executive staff for fixing. The employees receive reports on what actions will be taken and are given updates as plans are implemented.

Some very good ideas come from these sessions. Once solutions are implemented, employees feel motivated. They have had a say in the outcome of company plans.

Another positive result is that cross-functional groups get to meet each other and hear the issues affecting employees across the company.

Encouraging and creating meetings like this are essential. Teamwork doesn't just happen. You have to bring people together. You have to give them a common goal.

CHAPTER TWELVE

RED FLAGS

Monday, Dec. 21

Roger

I called Patricia. You can imagine her reaction.

I told her she should try to get the next plane to Reno, the airport closest to Lake Tahoe.

Patricia

The phone rang just before noon (9:00 a.m. West coast time).

I was surprised when I heard Roger's voice on the line. I knew he had been skiing with Nick at Lake Tahoe.

But why was he calling me?

I knew soon: Roger told me he never connected with Nick. I immediately heard warning bells in my head. Then the waves of panic started. It took all my energy to keep the panic at bay and concentrate on what Roger was saying. My heart was pounding so hard I was sure he could hear it over the phone. There was a terrible ringing in my ears.

I had never fainted in my life, but I came close that morning. Somehow I started to focus on the conversation.

When I heard Nick had missed a meeting and left no word, this was an immediate red flag. Something was very wrong. Nick would never miss a meeting without letting someone know.

The search for my husband became a team effort at that moment.

Nick, Jr.

They were going to try and locate him before they called and worried my mother, you know? At first they thought maybe he got into an accident on the way to the resort.

Roger was the first contact. He called my mother and said my father's bags were still there in the hotel room—but no sign of my father.

Once Roger called and he was really concerned about it, then we realized something was probably wrong.

Patricia

Breaking the news to my 23-year-old son, who was by my side, was incredibly difficult. Life can change in a split second. He was getting ready to spend the day at the beach with his girlfriend Ashley.

No more.

We had to find his father.

Recently, I saw a movie called "Sliding Doors" with Gwyneth Paltrow.

Basically, the movie shows you have many options when you're presented with a problem or a situation. The outcome just depends on which way you go.

I feel like I had three options that Monday morning when Roger called.

I could have said to Roger, "It's just Nick. You know—he does this all the time. He'll call; don't worry about it. Just go back to San Francisco, go to your office, I'll call you when I hear from him."

Had I taken that road, Nick probably wouldn't be here today.

I could have been the kind of person that would have just crumbled, rolled into a fetal position and sobbed. Honestly, I would have liked to have done that.

But I didn't. I'm the kind of person who just puts all the emotions aside and does what I have to do.

I think Nick was 100 percent certain on that mountain I was going to do everything I could possibly do to find him. And I think that, in some way, that had to be a comfort to him. He knew the kind of person I was.

He knew, whatever it took, I would find him—or I would die trying. I think that probably did offer him some kind of comfort.

Linda

Once we figured Nick was probably in an accident I went in to John Hagedorn, the CFO.

I said, "John, I can't find Nick anywhere. Here's the situation." I went over what we had figured out.

He said, "I will handle Nick's staff meeting at 10."

He let the staff know people were looking for Nick.

Joyce

I was getting ready for work. Patricia called, and she was hysterical. I could barely understand what she was trying to tell me. But she finally got it out: Roger had called her, and Nick was missing. She didn't know if he was dead or alive. I could hardly understand her, because she was so hysterical.

He hadn't been in his room, his bed hadn't been slept in. She was hysterical. What was she going to do? How could she live without him? You know—the normal emotions you go through.

He was missing, and they had had a horrendous snowstorm. Friday was the last time anyone had seen him or spoken with him.

I tell you, I was probably not as emotional as Patricia, but when you've known somebody that long—I was hysterical myself by the time we got off the phone.

Perseverance:

Have Faith and Keep Pushing

My good friend Al Siders is the epitome of perseverance. Al has started three companies. He lives in Chicago and gets offers to move to various places in the U.S. for new jobs, but for family reasons has chosen to stay in the Chicago area.

His alternative?

Start another company. Al starts his companies in the Chicago area and, when the time is right, sells them. It takes a lot of faith in yourself to start new companies, but he knows if he can make it work, the family doesn't have to move.

His latest company is Network Data Systems; I am on their board of directors.

Network Data focuses on providing high-end technical consulting services to large enterprise customers. Recently, the market for technical consulting was very tough. Al had to re-engineer the cost side of the company in order to get back to break-even profitability.

This kind of work isn't new to Al. During the second year of the company, computer hardware sales margins became very thin and Al re-engineered the business to focus on technical consulting.

Throughout all of his efforts Al has focused heavily on integrity and on doing the right thing for the people in the company.

Network Data is moving back to profitability thanks

to Al. He never gives up. He can be relied upon to do whatever it takes to make his business successful.

CHAPTER THIRTEEN

THE FIGHT

Monday, Dec. 21

Patricia

Together we manned three phones. Somehow, we also managed to keep my eighty-six-year-old father completely unaware Nick was missing.

I could handle only one emergency at a time.

Roger checked with the highway patrol one more time. This time they asked for the license plate number. With this information, they could use the computer to determine within fifteen seconds if the car had been towed. When he called me for the tag number, my mind went blank.

Several phone calls and many wasted minutes later, I finally tracked down the tag number through the hotel. For once, luck: Nick had written it on his hotel registration form. I passed this information on to Roger.

I called the hospitals in Tahoe to see if a "John Doe" had been admitted. I thought perhaps he had been injured skiing and had forgotten to carry his identification.

No. No "John Doe."

Nick hadn't told anyone where he was skiing. I called the hotel and asked for a list of all ski resorts within a twenty-minute drive—I didn't think Nick would drive farther than that from the hotel.

My son and I split this list up, called the resorts and asked if any ski accidents had been reported.

No. No accidents reported.

Nick never seems to have any cash on him. I called the bank, hoping he had charged his lift tickets.

No. He withdrew $200 from an ATM at a Tahoe bank. He had cash.

We asked if any cars had been left on the resort parking lots.

At last—yes! But then, to my horror, I was told any cars left on the lot after closing are towed; license plate numbers are not recorded. I still don't understand this policy.

So now we had a second problem: Where was Nick's car?

Linda

Roger was calling around to see if Nick had been towed or was in an accident. I was calling resorts to see if his car was in a parking lot still.

That's when the security guard said you know, they tow the cars if the parking lots aren't cleared.

I said, "Oh, *really?*"

"Yes," he said. "If they aren't out by the time they close the resort, then they call and they get them all towed."

Meanwhile, Patricia kept making calls, and Roger was on his way back to Tahoe.

"I'm going up there," he said. "Just in case."

He was very concerned when he was driving up there. He stopped at a gas station, and he took off with the hose still in his tank.

Roger

I had talked with their son, Nickie. I told Nickie, "You need to get your mom on the first plane out here, because I don't know what's going on."

We agreed she should get the first flight she could into Reno.

Patricia

As Roger dealt with Squaw, I mustered other support.

The first person I called was Joyce Canzionieri. We have been best friends—more like sisters (without the family baggage)—for twenty-nine years. She lived in the Bay Area, and I asked her to stay by the phone and be ready to leave on a moment's notice.

I still had faith Nick would be found alive; I knew Joyce could get to him long before I could. I wanted Nick to see a familiar face when he was found, and I desperately wanted her support when I arrived.

Next, I called my dear friend Maryann Schoulz, a travel agent. I needed her to get me and my son on a flight to Reno, the closest major airport to Tahoe—no small task, three days before Christmas.

I said over and over, "What am I going to do, Maryann? What am I going to do?"

God love her, she gave me the pep talk I needed.

Finally, I had to make the hardest call: Our daughter, Jennifer. I didn't want to worry her until I knew more, but finally I had no choice. It was not easy.

Maryann Schoulz

Patricia called me at work to tell me what had happened. I was working as a travel agent in New Jersey at the time. She called and told me Nick was missing—that was the first phone call.

I remember saying, "Don't count him out."

They didn't seem to be offering her a lot of hope at that point.

She said, "I don't know what to do. We've never talked about anything like this."

She meant, if he was gone.

"What would I do?" she said.

"Don't even go there," I said. "Don't count him out yet. If there's any way, I know he'll survive this."

I think that's what she was saying to me in that first conversation: How would she bring his body back?

Roger

Even now, I'm still thinking "auto accident." I got Nick's license plate number from Patricia and called the highway patrol again. I called the Truckee office of the California Highway Patrol and spoke to one person for at least the third time.

I said, "Look—I'm desperate. We have no record of the vehicle, he's not in the hospital, there's no accident. Are you sure you don't have anything?"

"Well, let me just try one more thing," she said.

It wasn't more than 30 seconds.

"The car was towed from Squaw Valley at 2:00 a.m. Sunday morning," she said.

Talk about a REAL cold chill going down your back. I said, "Oh, my god."

Until that moment, the thought of him being lost wasn't even a thought.

But now he wasn't just missing.

He was lost.

Patricia

Nick's car was at the Squaw Valley resort. I hadn't called there; it was more than twenty minutes from Nick's hotel.

But apparently, that's where Nick had gone to ski.

Three days ago.

Teamwork:

Teams Are Vital

Quite often in companies the corporate executives espouse teamwork, and expect it from their employees.

But it is very difficult to expect teamwork if the executives don't set the standard.

Teamwork starts at the top.

There are usually conflicts among the various organizations in a company. Executives must work together to resolve these conflicts.

For example: engineering and manufacturing. Quite often engineers design products that are difficult to manufacture, or that use hard-to-obtain parts. Why?

Because the engineers want the best possible product, or the product that is most elegant. So it is necessary for the engineering and manufacturing groups to work together to design products that are easy to manufacture *and* are designed to satisfy customers.

As a CEO it is necessary to make sure each person on the executive team understands working together as a team is not an option—it is a requirement.

A good approach to instill teamwork is to work together to define the mission, goals, and objectives of the company with the CEO as the facilitator. This usually involves several weeks of off-site meetings to work through the company's key areas of focus. It certainly involves all key executives that report to the CEO.

It is necessary to listen to everyone and capture the

main ideas. It is also necessary to allow lots of discussion about each goal and objective.

Goals are longer-term—three to five years out—such as "Achieve annual revenues of $500M by 2005."

Objectives are set yearly in order to achieve the longer-term goal.

Normally, there is conflict between various functional organizations. Objectives for each organization are at odds with each other since budgets and resources are limited. Goals and objectives must be prioritized and resources allocated accordingly. This occurs through planning sessions or working sessions with all executives present. The CEO must hear everyone's input and decide on priorities.

Through this approach, it is possible to set corporate objectives and objectives for each department. To accomplish the objectives the departments must work together.

If the executives work together, employees see the example and are much more likely to work together.

And executives who do not work together effectively? The CEO can *not* let them be part of the team.

CHAPTER FOURTEEN

THE BEGINNING, THE END

Monday, Dec. 21
Morning

Roger

His car was towed?

The problem is, if you haven't been through this kind of situation, you don't even know the right questions to ask.

I called the Squaw Valley ski resort immediately.

"You have a skier lost there," I said. "You need to get out there and start looking for him."

They weren't ready to start that quickly, however. They wanted to hear from his wife. I gave their number to Patricia and she was on the phone to them within five minutes.

I got back in my car and headed for Tahoe. Just to be there, just in case.

Galeen Stratton
Dependable Tow
Tahoe

Getting towed from the ski resorts? It's pretty common.

If it snows at night, they have to do snow removal in the parking lots. They tow the cars from 11:00 p.m. to 6:00 a.m.

There are hotels all around the Squaw parking lot. There are condominiums, there's a post office, there are shops. There are bars there, too. It can be really hard to know where the car came from.

The resorts clear the lots for safety reasons so people can get in and park the next day easily, and so they're not tripping and falling in the parking lot.

They also don't want to be hitting the cars with the plows while they're trying to clean the lots. That has happened.

Linda

Roger called me on his way to Tahoe. He said, "Linda—they've found the car. They towed it from Squaw."

I talked to the people at Squaw, and then Patricia.

I think we all talked to them.

They told Roger they would not send out search and rescue until they had talked to the wife.

That's what they said. "We're not going to dispatch anyone until we talk to the wife."

Patricia

At 10:00 a.m. I received another call from Roger. Squaw Valley was not cooperating.

The ski patrol was reluctant to send out search parties based solely on a car being towed. They also wanted to know if we had a stable marriage, and if Nick was a flake. Apparently they had the same crazy ideas Roger initially had—was Nick out somewhere, having a lark? They didn't want to go out on a wild goose chase. Search and rescue is costly and very time-consuming; they wanted additional proof he was missing.

I was informed I had to file a missing person's report with the sheriff's department before any further action could be taken.

So I called the sheriff. As kindly as possible they told me not to expect to find my husband alive. They also told me I should speak with someone about how to bring a body back from the Lake Tahoe area. Apparently, the nighttime temperatures had hit an all-time low; the chances of someone surviving a blizzard at those temperatures for two-and-one-half days were very slim.

Body? Nick?

Until that moment I had not really considered the possibility my husband could be dead. I had been prepared to deal with an injury—but not his death.

No, I was too young to be a widow, and my children were not going to be fatherless.

I was more determined than ever to find him alive.

Roger

When they tow somebody out of one of the parking lots,

they have to make a record of it.

That's something that—my lord—nobody knows unless you've gone through this. That would be the very first thing I'd ask—today—if somebody were missing and I didn't know what ski area they were at. I'd call in and say, "Have you towed a vehicle?" You wouldn't have to call every tow truck company. You'd call the sheriff's department: "Do you have a record of this vehicle having been towed?"

I couldn't have done it without the license plate number. The person's name isn't enough—absolutely not. There's no reason for them to track down the names and have those available.

Their assumption is the person's okay, and the person's going to come claim their vehicle because they were just irresponsible and went out partying with somebody and left their vehicle there.

Nick, Jr.

We talked to one of the ski patrol, the head of the ski patrol. They were being pretty frank about it, saying in that particular part of the country, these type of storms are pretty notorious and every year, "x" amount of people go missing on these slopes and "x" amount of people are never found.

After a day had gone by, I was prepared to go with my mother to just kind of… prepare for the worst. That's what I had expected. I was preparing for that. I was trying to be as supportive as possible because my mother was not doing very well.

Patricia

When I met Nick, I knew that was what I wanted. I wanted

to spend the rest of my life with him.

Together, we worked very hard as a team to create that kind of family, that kind of life. Every decision we ever made while we were married, we made together, as a team.

Even when he was lost on that mountain we were working as a team. We were doing what came naturally. He was doing whatever it took to keep himself alive, and I was doing whatever it took to find him.

And it worked.

I was able to put the emotions away and to do everything I could to find him: to make the calls, to track down the sheriff, to track down the ATM records.

The emotions? Truthfully, I don't know how you can even put them on the page. I don't think anyone can come close to understanding the emotions I was going through.

When that sheriff told me I probably was not going to find my husband alive and I needed to come and prepare myself, the bottom went out for me.

Life stopped. Even if it was just for a second, my whole life stopped. I wondered how in the world would I ever, ever be able to live without him.

Galeen Stratton
Dependable Tow
Tahoe

I wouldn't want to be lost out there. It is very easy to get lost out there. People just don't realize how EASY it is to get yourself turned around out there.

We snowmobile a lot. We snowmobile on trails we Jeep on in the summertime. The surrounding areas are familiar to me, but when the snow falls, everything changes. He ended up going in circles? I'm not surprised. As he's moving, the snow is wiping away his tracks. He probably didn't know he was going in circles.

That's something that's regularly taught up here in the schools: winter survival. Every year, the kids get a book, "Hug a Tree: A Winter Survival Guide for Primary Grades." They teach the kids all these things. They start in kindergarten, and they get it every year in school.

Nick

At 9:00 a.m. I needed to stop and rest. I found a tree to lean against and, unbelievably, discovered my skis! Amazing. After two days, I was back to the place where I had first left my skis.

Using a technique learned in Marine survival training, I decided to make sure I was moving in the right direction.

Breaking a straight branch from a tree, I stuck it into the snow perpendicular to the ground. I marked the tip of the shadow the branch made with smaller sticks, making the marks every five minutes. The line connecting the shadow tips pointed west. This confirmed I was moving in a north-easterly direction. Staying on this course should get me to the ski lifts.

As the morning progressed, the sun grew brighter, and the wind began to die down. My body became less and less cold, and my will to make it to safety grew stronger every moment.

Patricia

What prepared me to be the kind of person who would search for Nick on that mountain?

A lot of things. Anybody who has been a teacher for years never enters a classroom unprepared. That helped.

Another contributor was just being Nick's wife. We started out as a military family, then a corporate one. I was prepared for the next move. I was prepared for the last-minute dinner party he would bring home.

He was on the road a lot when he was in the corporate world, and I ran the house. That's just the role I had. That's me.

Positive Attitude:

It Can Only Help

In 1976, I had already left the Marine Corps and was at home in Hubbard, Ohio, considering my next move.

During my visit I had the opportunity to discuss career opportunities with one of my dad's customers—and long-time friend—Bob Gibson. He was a systems engineer for IBM in Youngstown, Ohio.

Bob told me I should consider a career with IBM. That day he was on his way to Sharon, Pennsylvania, to install a new operating system for a division of Westinghouse. He invited me to tag along.

We arrived at the customer site and were greeted by the data processing manager for the site. This manager brought us to the data center—a room built behind a glass wall for all to see. It had a raised floor for good air flow, several mainframe computers, disk drives and spinning tape drives.

Bob began to install the system upgrade and took me step-by-step through the process, including loading the new program via a card reader, querying the operating system, and running a test job. The whole process was very interesting, and the customers gave Bob the run of their shop and a good dose of appreciation and respect.

On the way back from Sharon, Bob and I discussed the different types of jobs available at IBM. My skills best fit salesman. I was enthusiastic, unafraid, and could explain technical concepts in terms people could understand because of my background as Avionics Division Officer in the Marines.

I asked Bob how I could become part of IBM. He gave me the name and phone number of the branch manager in Baltimore, near our home.

Branch managers at the time in IBM had status because each branch was normally responsible for hundreds of millions of dollars in sales revenue. Each branch manager had a full staff, including a private secretary.

Thus, when I called the branch manager and he answered his own phone, I was surprised. I quickly told him my background and why I wanted to work for IBM. I think my positive attitude and enthusiasm surprised him. I spoke to him as if I deserved a job with IBM because I believed in myself and was excited about what I had seen at Westinghouse.

The branch manager asked me to come to his office the next day, Tuesday. I met with him and every manager in his office that day, and then went to the regional HQ next day to meet many more people. I started work at IBM Friday of the same week. I was later told by the branch manager that he took a chance on me because of my attitude and enthusiasm. He did not have authority to hire any more sales people that year, so I had to interview with his boss for approval.

My positive attitude served me well, and I had a very successful eight-year career with IBM.

CHAPTER FIFTEEN

MAN OF SNOW AND ICE

Monday, Dec. 21
Morning

Nick

At around 11:00 a.m., the sun was peeking over the mountaintop. I was completely covered with snow and ice, and needed to rest and get my bearings.

I arrived at an area that was windswept, flat, and wide open. There was a dead tree at the center. I walked to the tree and leaned against it, soaking up rays of sunlight, actually feeling some warmth.

I thought I saw the tops of ski lifts to my left and what appeared to be a wooden deck directly in front of me. Both the ski lifts and the wooden deck were far off into the distance, and the terrain to get to them was steep and treacherous. There were many large rocks with several deep ravines between me and civilization.

However, my spirits were high. What could be better than relaxing in the sun, getting a suntan and planning my route to the top of the mountain? My plan was to rest for two hours, let the snow and ice melt from my clothing, and climb to safety. Hopefully, I could be there by nightfall.

An airplane flew overhead. I waved my ski poles wildly over my head. Deep down, I knew the plane was much too high to see anything. I waved, regardless. Later, I saw a small two-engine plane flying at a lower altitude. I tried again. That plane also continued on its course.

Periodically, I began to scream for help at the top of my lungs.

There was no return response, but I had come too far to even think about giving up.

Leaning against that dead tree in the sun, I was gaining strength and warmth. The majority of the snow and ice melted from my clothes, and my face felt sunburned. With the exception of my feet most of my body finally felt very warm.

Patricia

Once I filed the missing person's report with the sheriff, I immediately got back on the phone with the Squaw Valley ski patrol.

Now they were satisfied. They began an all-mountain search, and approximately fifty employees began an immediate in-house and boundary search.

Meanwhile, they had questions. They needed additional information about my husband's skiing ability. My son, Nicholas, and my godson, John Canzionieri, were able to help with these questions. Both had skied with Nick and knew his capabilities. They wanted to know which slopes my husband normally skied, if he skied moguls, and if he took risks. This information enabled search and rescue to target the search area. Both snowmobiles and snow cats were then dispatched for an out-of-bounds search.

That was all I could do; everything was then out of my hands. All I could do was wait by the phone and pray.

I did have one more call. I knew I couldn't keep this latest information from my daughter Jennifer any longer.

Once again, I asked a best friend for help. Peg Lawrence and I have been friends for over twenty years. I told Peg everything, and asked her to please go to Jennifer's office and tell her face-to-face what had happened to her father.

She did.

Then Jennifer and I talked. I supplied all the missing details and promised to call as soon as I heard any news. I convinced her to go home with Peg. Plans would have to be made later, but at that time all she could really do was wait and pray.

Almost two years later Jennifer revealed to me she was not as optimistic as I was. She really thought her father would not be found alive.

Jennifer Williams

I was at work. My mom sent Peg Lawrence over to tell me my father was lost. That's all we knew—that he was missing.

At that moment, I remember feeling it was the worst day of my life. It was two days, three days before Christmas. My mother always strived to make Christmas a wonderful holiday for all of us. My thoughts were "Christmas will be horrendous from this point out."

I left work and I went to my mom's best friend's house. I was trying to make plane reservations to get to either Tahoe or Florida, depending on what my mother wanted me to do.

Thomas Blanchard
Financial Advisor
Salomon Smith Barney

Nick and Patricia have been my clients for years.

Patricia called and told me what had happened. She goes, "I'm not sure if he's alive or not. They're searching for him, and it doesn't look good." It had been a couple of days.

"I'm going to go out there," she says.

She was very distraught, some trembling in her voice, some crying. She thought this was probably it.

Patricia had a couple of concerns. For one thing, most of my dealings had been with Nick, although Patricia was also on the accounts. She needed to know if she would have access to the accounts if there was an emergency. I assured her, yes, that's fine.

I don't get many calls like that. I get calls that clients have passed away, but this one was a shocker. Just knowing Nick as long as I did, and how athletic he was—the guy's in great shape, he skis all the time—I'm thinking, "What are the chances of *that* happening?"

Nick

At 12:30 p.m., I heard what I thought were snowmobiles. I began to scream in their direction and was sure someone was yelling back. Then the sound of the snowmobiles retreated and I wasn't quite sure what to think. Were there search parties out looking for me? Or were the snowmobiles just people out having fun and not really looking for anyone?

The sounds died away. I kept walking.

Jimmy King

I'm the mountain manager at Squaw Valley.

When someone is missing on the mountain, my people always meet quickly and plan our response.

We grade it, 1 to 10, in three minutes. Depending on that grading, the more resources we put out there.

Nick got an 8.8.

It started getting bad the day he disappeared. The next day it got worse.

Most of our storms are not cold. But the storm that weekend was extremely cold. Our storms come from the north—but usually our winds come from the south, south-west—not the north, like that weekend.

We had no clue someone was out there.

Because of the weather factor, and because time was of the essence, I decided to order a ship—a helicopter.

"Boy," I thought, "we've got a window of weather. It could be changing in the next 6 to 10 hours—let's just order a helicopter right now."

So I did—a Jet Ranger five-person helicopter. I made sure it was fully loaded with fuel.

The helicopter can do a lot, but it can't do everything. We sent out snowmobiles, but because of the terrain, we can only send snowmobiles to certain areas of our wilderness land.

Two teams of two skiers were put on alert.

We went up the mountain.

Nick, Jr.

My mother and I were going to fly out. There was some es-
tate stuff we had to take care of, in the event my father was not...
going to be found, which is what we were planning for.

I didn't know if we were going to see him, or if we were... I
don't know. I just know things were pretty messed up and we
were on our way out to California. We were on our way west.

We spoke with my sister and my grandfather, who was going
to stay in Florida. My mother and I were going to try to get closer
to this... you know, this accident.

I'm literally on the way out the door. That's when the phone
rang. Literally. I had my bags packed. We were going to go, to
see... get closer. As we were walking out the door, the phone
rang.

Positive Attitude:

Hope, For No Reason

There were many times I could have had a negative outlook. But I chose to approach each day with the attitude I was blessed to be alive, and thanked God for each day.

In business, there are many situations where it seems all is lost. But keeping a positive attitude in front of customers and business partners just may make the difference.

When I was with IBM, I worked with Doug Munro, VP of Manufacturing Information Systems for Ward Machinery Corp. Doug always maintained a positive attitude, no matter what.

One time, a new systems installation went bad for a variety of reasons. I was the salesman on the account. We were installing a new computer and new database system.

Our systems engineer planned everything to the finest detail. However, when the new database was tied together with the new computer, there were some bad surprises.

The computer was supposed to be installed on a Saturday so we could have Sunday to test the new database and go "live" for manufacturing applications on Monday. We began early Saturday morning after the last manufacturing run.

First the printer didn't work properly. We had to reconfigure the print driver.

Then the database records became out of sync, so the Bills of Material were not printing the information we would need to begin manufacturing on Monday.

It seemed endless.

Throughout the process, Doug maintained a positive attitude and kept all of his team and mine focused and positive about accomplishing our task. Sunday at noon we had a decision to make: either complete the installation and continue to rework the database, or fall back on the old system. Doug made the decision to press forward.

We made the deadline—with two hours to spare.

Doug gained the respect of his team, and the IBM team as well, all because of his positive, "will-do" attitude.

Nick Williams

Nick and Patricia

Jennifer, Nickie, Nick and Patricia

Nick, Nickie and Patricia

Backside of Granite Mountain

Hotel in Truckee

Bob and Joyce

Nick and Roger Dorf

Nick and Jimmy King

Dr. Bunke

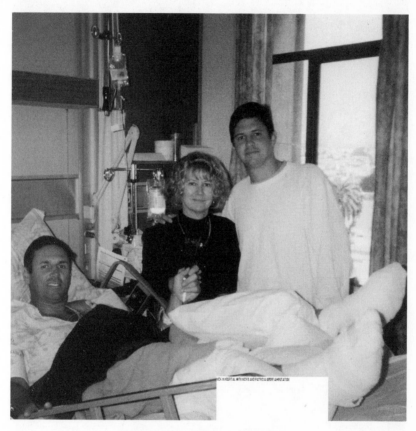

Nick, Patricia and Nickie

Nick and Dr. Bunke

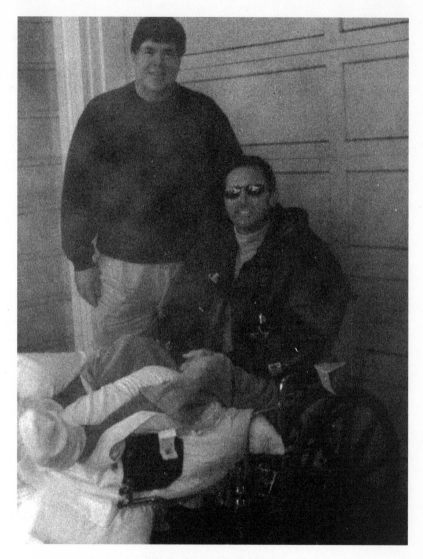

Rick Drew and Nick

CHAPTER SIXTEEN

TURNAROUND

Monday, Dec. 21
Noon

Jimmy King

Nick says he was screaming at the top of his lungs? I bet he was.

It worked. The snowmobiles heard him. They heard him the first time they came by.

But they still didn't know where he was.

Sound travels incredibly well over water, and almost as well over snow. It can travel incredible distances. You could not figure out where the sound came from, but you could hear it.

So they heard Nick, but they had no idea where the sound was coming from.

He was in one area we never had a crew go down. Never in the history of Squaw Valley. Nobody has gone as far as him. We've never sent skiers that far.

Still, everybody was feeling great relief when we had voice contact. That meant he was conscious; we knew he was moving around.

Nick

One of the snowmobile guys said, "We hear you." I started crying. I'm just sobbing.

Patricia

Around 12:30 p.m. West coast time, two searchers riding snowmobiles on the back side of the Granite Chief peak found my husband.

They were following standard search and rescue procedure by stopping repeatedly and shutting off the motors. They would then call out in an effort to receive voice recognition. It was during one of these stops they heard Nick calling out. It was impossible to reach him because the terrain was too steep.

They brought in the helicopter.

Jimmy King

We flew to Nick's location, guided by the snowmobile trackers.

The wind was blowing right at him. It was blowing out of the southwest.

As we flew over, I spotted his footprints first, before I saw him. They were coming from down below.

We landed.

The helicopter pilot never got out. I got out.

This guy comes running up to me. I'm thinking, "He's in better shape than I am!"

I asked him, "Are you Nick Williams?"

He was running down this hill at me—running!

We talked about his feet a little bit. I said, "You've got some foot problems, don't you."

He said, "Yeah, they froze."

His survival?

I think it was very questionable. I think it all depended on his own resources.

He saved himself. We aligned ourselves to give each other the best opportunity to find each other. If he hadn't kept himself alive, I don't know if we ever would have found him, to tell you the truth.

Would a lot of people have made it through that? No way. Absolutely not.

Longest time anyone was ever missing on the mountain and found alive? Since I've been here and working on these types of rescues—over 20 years—we've never had anybody out there as long as Nick was. He was there the longest because we didn't know he was out there.

Things just sometimes work out for the better. We were planning on the worst, but everything lined up.

Nick

At 1:00 p.m., just as I was preparing to resume my climb, the sounds of the snowmobiles returned. This time they came closer. I couldn't see them, but could hear them more clearly than before. I screamed for five or ten minutes with no response.

Finally, someone yelled back. "We hear you. We hear you." I

was elated. I knew my rescue was imminent and the long, steep final climb was not going to be necessary.

About ten minutes later, a small helicopter circled over my position several times looking for a place to land. I began to cry and thank God.

I knew I had made it.

The helicopter landed about 200 yards away from me in a flat area. Adrenaline pumping, I ran as fast as I could toward the helicopter, not even thinking about my feet.

It appeared to be a two-man helicopter and one person got out, Jimmy King.

As I approached, he was on his walkie-talkie saying, "This isn't the victim. This can't be the victim. This is someone who has been snow-shoeing or hiking." He asked my name. I said, "Nick Williams."

I wasn't sure he believed me, but he said into the walkie-talkie, "This is the victim." He asked if anything was wrong with me. I told him nothing was wrong except my feet were frozen. He nodded and looked me over once more, then told me to get into the helicopter.

I got in and we lifted off, heading for the Squaw Valley helipad. An ambulance was waiting for us there.

The first thing I asked for was a cell phone.

Teamwork:

Make and Use a Good Team

When I was Vice President of North American Sales at AT&T Paradyne, John Mitcham was the CEO.

John had a vision.

He wanted our company to win the Malcolm Baldridge National Quality Award. He spent a year implementing quality measures, trying to get the company to step up to the challenge.

It wasn't enough. John took drastic action.

He appointed a team of executives from each key area of the company to develop and implement "Total Quality Management," or "TQM," in AT&T Paradyne. The long-term goal was clear: winning the Baldridge.

The team consisted of me, Ed Thompson (VP of Manufacturing), John Corroneous (VP of Customer Service), Doug Hotchkiss (Controller), Clete Gardenhauer (Chief Technical Officer), and Lee Beaumont (Director of Development) from Bell Labs.

We each stepped out of our current jobs for the duty— in my case, eight months—and our time was assigned 100 percent to implementing TQM.

In addition, John dedicated three percent of the company—100 people—to the effort. We trained together, set goals and objectives, and met daily to adjust priorities and follow up with others in the company.

The team worked very closely together and accomplished many objectives in a short period of time. We trained 2,500 people, met with customers to explain the process, started continuous improvement projects in every manager's area, and set 10 key benchmarks for our quality program. We checked the benchmarks with our customers to be sure the benchmarks were relevant to them.

Working with the team was a pleasure. We could fill in for each other and we were looked up to by many in the company. Although team members represented different areas of the company, we put away our biases and set about learning how to have a positive effect on the company as a whole.

We succeeded.

TQM became a way of life for employees of AT&T Paradyne and we won an AT&T award for quality.

I have rarely had the opportunity to work with a team that was so well-connected with one another. The feeling was truly amazing. We knew we could rely on each other and we also knew we could accomplish the most challenging objectives.

Why?

Because we were all committed to the same mission and were given the authority and responsibility to act on behalf of the company. It was one of the most rewarding experiences of my business career.

CHAPTER SEVENTEEN

THE END

Monday, Dec. 21

Patricia

Maryann somehow got seats for Nicholas and me on a flight from Tampa, Florida, to Reno, Nevada. We were going to claim my husband's body.

At 4:30 p.m. Florida time the phone rang.

I was in the bedroom packing my suitcase. My son answered the phone. I heard him say "Who is this?"

Then he broke down and began to cry.

Nick, Jr.

I answered the phone, and it was my father on the phone, calling from the back of an ambulance. I was prepared for the worst, thinking, "Okay, it's been this long. There's no way they were going to be able to get him."

But it was him, in the back of the ambulance, saying, "Hey, how are you?" I dropped the phone and started crying. My mom grabbed the phone. From there, she took over. It was like I was taking over up until that point, and after that, she took over.

Patricia

I rushed to the phone and heard my husband's voice telling me he was alive and well. He was crying, too.

An attendant got on the phone and told me Nick was in good spirits and appeared to be fine except for cold feet.

I called my daughter and we both had a good cry.

Roger, who was on his way to Tahoe, was next on my list. He was filling his car at a gas station in Sacramento when I reached him on his cell phone. He was so excited he drove off with the hose still attached to his car.

Roger was the first to arrive in Tahoe, just in time to meet Nick.

Never were two friends so glad to see each other.

Since Nick seemed fine—other than his cold feet—we decided I would fly into Reno alone and bring him back to Florida for Christmas. My son would stay and care for his grandfather and wait for his sister to arrive.

What an incredible relief. Life, finally, could go on as planned.

Nick

I called my family from the ambulance. My twenty-three-year-old son, Nicholas, answered. I was so excited. I said, "Hello, Nickie!"

"Who is this?" he said. He sounded suspicious.

I said, "Nickie, it's me—Dad—I'm OK."

Then he broke. He said, "Dad you're alive, you're alive, I love you, Dad," and began to cry. I was sobbing when Patricia got on the phone and said, "Oh my God, you're alive, thank God." She began to cry also.

During the short ambulance ride to Lake Tahoe Forest Hospital, the attendant covered me with blankets and gave me water.

As we arrived at the hospital, I stood up and walked into the emergency room. The attending physician began to examine me and asked me to describe my injuries.

My only concern was my frozen feet, I told him. The doctor shook his head as if he didn't believe me, and then tried to remove my ski boots.

The boots did not come off; they were frozen to my feet.

Joyce

Patricia called and said they found him and she was going to fly out.

I called my boyfriend at work and said, "We have to get up there." I wanted at least somebody to be up there when he got to the hospital. The weather was really bad so it took a while, but we got there a while later.

Nobody went to work that whole day. Everybody was just trying to figure out what was going on.

It was a really horrible time. It was really bad for all of us.

Nick

Hospital personnel moved me to another room with a whirlpool bath, sat me on the edge and put my feet—boots and all—into the lukewarm water. While sitting there, a nurse asked if I were hungry. I said I was starving. She brought me an egg salad sandwich, vegetables and hot chicken soup.

No hospital food ever tasted better.

After I had been in the whirlpool about an hour, Roger arrived. This was a very emotional reunion. With tears in his eyes, he hugged me and told me he had been afraid he would never see me again.

We each had a story to tell about the past three days, and spent some time telling it.

Then, true friend, he went to get me a large cheeseburger with fries and a milk shake.

Roger

Relieved? I was in tears. I was so relieved he was alive. It was so awful.

Nick, Jr.

It was pretty traumatic.

I think as time goes by you tend to black a lot of that stuff out. The most vivid thing in my mind from that stage is that phone call. And dropping the phone. I think probably to this day it was the happiest moment in my life. I don't know how else you can explain it. You go from the worst thing that could ever happen to basically a miracle, I guess. I don't know. Most of the people that lived in that area at that time were describing it as that.

From that point on, things in life were pretty easy to deal with. Once you go through something like that, it's easier to deal with things.

Dr. Howard Boone
Lake Tahoe Community Hospital

We used to get an average of several rescued skiers a year in the ER. It seemed like it was always when I was on call.

The amount of damage they get?

It depends on the weather more than anything.

You could be out three or four days in nice weather and it's no sweat. But if it's brutally cold, you can get into terrible trouble overnight.

Persistence:

The Only Way to Reach the Finish Line

I could have given up at any time. Then, nothing else I had done would have mattered; I would have failed.

You see the importance of this every day in business.

When I was President of Network Access Solutions, the key performance metric was the time required to deliver our product: high-speed lines for Internet access.

Most companies were unable to deliver these high-speed lines within 90 days. There were many reasons for this, including line distance and the condition of the copper line. For us, the main issue was a key service provider, Verizon: they were not cooperative. This gave us frustrated customers and frustrated employees. We had no control over how Verizon would work with us to provide service.

We had to find a better way.

This was going to take strong leadership. Bill Boykin was the solution. Bill didn't have telecommunications experience, but he knew something about leadership. He had been Vice President of Operations at a manufacturing company—and before that was the Commanding Officer of two nuclear submarines!

"I was unwilling to accept the status quo and the excuses involved in failures to take responsibility," says Bill. "In order to make those reductions happen, I had to evaluate processes and organizations, find the weaknesses, and resolve them. I had to change the organization so there would be responsibility across all capabilities for improvement in efficiency."

It was familiar territory.

"I tried to use in the civilian world some of the techniques I had used to develop highly-performing teams in the military," says Bill.

When he joined us as Vice President of Operations, he quickly went to work to understand the situation. He found the process of providing the lines was taking an average of 68 days. He broke the process down into steps and discovered the biggest chunk of that time—about 38 days—was due to Verizon. He broke it down further and found much of that time was spent in getting a Verizon customer service representative to install the line.

"It took some persistence," says Bill. "The people involved were convinced they were doing the job as best as it could be done. The problem was not them, it was 'someone else.' It was 'them.'"

But Bill was not willing to accept the excuse "It's their fault."

"We formed teams to investigate each failure, resolve it, and improve customer satisfaction," says Bill.

He began to track each step of the process, day by day, including the steps that were the responsibility of Verizon. He made a commitment to reduce the time to set up a line. Armed with data from each step of the process, he held weekly meetings with Verizon and began to set objectives with them for cycle time reductions.

He also held his own people accountable for their part of the process.

"People resisted for a while, until they understood the goals," says Bill. "I had to set very clear goals and expectations. I had to make the environment an environment of open communications, where people were not afraid to speak up and voice their concerns and opinions, and their need for help and change."

The environment became one of support throughout, he says, and a competitive environment where each part of the organization wanted to perform for the other parts.

The result: Within four months we reduced the installation time from 64 to 30 days.

Bill knew there must be a better way, and he didn't quit until he figured out what it was, and got us there.

CHAPTER EIGHTEEN

THE BEGINNING, THE END

Monday, Dec. 21
Evening

Joyce

Being so far away—that was so hard on Patricia. She was clear across the country. You're helpless anyway, but I think it makes you feel even more so. If she was here, it would have been different. Then we would have gotten in the car, we would have driven up, and—yes, we wouldn't have necessarily known anything, but at least we would have been there. I think it makes you feel a little differently when you're away from something like that.

Even when she was on the plane, flying back to Tahoe from Florida, there was still that uncertainty. What was she flying to? She knew he was "okay," but what was "okay"?

And she was by herself on the flight—that made it even worse. That's a very long flight.

Patricia

I left Tampa at 6:00 p.m. I had winter clothes borrowed from my son's girlfriend, and tranquilizers prescribed by Dr. Whiting, her father.

During a layover in Dallas, I called the hospital and checked on Nick.

Things had changed.

The diagnosis was worse, much worse. Now I learned Nick had severe frostbite and was in danger of losing his feet. Suddenly, my tranquilizer stopped working. I had managed to keep all my emotions under control so far, but now I was so scared I could hardly breathe. I knew my greatest challenge was still ahead.

Joyce

The entire drive up to Tahoe—it's three and a half or four hours—that whole time, I kept calling the hospital, but I couldn't get any information out of them. So when I got to the hospital, and they said, "Who are you?" I said, "I'm his sister," because I thought they weren't even going to let me in.

Poor Nick. He was still kind of confused. He said, "My sister?" and he's thinking, "My sister's in Ohio. How could she be here?"

I almost felt bad about that, because then he was expecting his sister. Oh well.

Roger

I was so tired.

I went and picked up Patricia. We had agreed she would come in on the first flight she could get to Reno. I think it was a 10:30 p.m. flight. This was after I had spent the afternoon there with Nick.

I slept on the floor of the airport waiting for her. I was totally wiped out. After she got in, we went back to the hospital.

Patricia

My plane landed in Reno at eleven o'clock. Roger met me at the airport—it was an emotional reunion. I had tried to be strong for everyone from the beginning, but now I let my guard down.

The final hour of my journey—up to the hospital in Tahoe— was the longest. I had been up for twenty-one hours and was in a daze. Roger tried to prepare me for Nick's condition, but nothing sunk in. I needed to see for myself.

When we stepped off the hospital elevator on Nick's floor, I turned to Roger.

"I don't know whether to hug and kiss him or to slap him," I said. Then I went to see my husband.

As I approached Nick's room, my friends Joyce and Bob were waiting. They had driven up from San Francisco. Joyce had told hospital security she was Nick's sister.

Joyce was not the only one trying to get to Nick. Even at that late hour, Nick's phone was being monitored by the hospital staff. Reporters had been calling and interviewing Nick all evening—

his story had even run on national news.

So he was a survivor. A hero. To me, he was my husband. And what a sight for my sore eyes he was. His right arm was hooked up to several IV tubes, including glucose and morphine. His feet were elevated and covered with a huge tent-like frame.

The protective tent was a critical part of his treatment, I learned. Nothing was to come into contact with Nick's feet—not even the sheet. Blisters were going to develop, I was told, and it was very important to keep the blistered skin intact as long as possible.

There was much hugging, kissing and crying. Nick looked happy and healthy. Under his three-day growth of beard, he was nicely tanned. It was hard to believe anything was wrong.

Until you saw his feet.

I peeked under the tent and had difficulty keeping my expression calm. His feet and toes were discolored and swollen. At that moment I realized we were in for the fight of our life.

Maryann

We were fixing dinner, and we saw him on television. That was the funniest thing. It was so good to see him. We knew he was okay. It was just so good to see him. He made some comment about being hungry.

Patricia

Decisions had to be made, by someone.

I knew it would have to be me. I was exhausted, but Nick was on morphine.

My first decision: To stay in Nick's room all night and never let him out of my sight.

It would be many weeks before I had a good night's sleep again. Nurses came in and out continuously. When the nurses weren't checking on Nick, I was. Every time I looked at his feet, I prayed for a miracle. I was glad when the morning nursing shift finally arrived and with them came the doctor.

Resourcefulness:

Use Your Network

Sometimes you can't do it alone—and you shouldn't. That's when it's time to call upon all your resources.

In 1981, I was promoted to Regional Marketing Representative in IBM's Mid-Atlantic region. It was my job to help our sales teams in several product areas, including the IBM 4300 mid-range computer and our large mainframe computers. The competitors of the day were Amdahl and NAS—two American companies selling computers manufactured in Japan. Their products were known as "Plug Compatible"; IBM peripherals and operating systems could run seamlessly plugged in to the foreign computer. These systems were offered at a lower price than the comparable IBM computers.

In many regions of the U.S., the competitors were having some success. Not in the Mid-Atlantic region. This was thanks to the efforts of Selby Wellman, my boss at the time. Selby devised a plan to attack Amdahl and NAS.

Here's how it worked:

We would go to a branch office in the region where there was a competitive threat. We would work with the branch manager and his team to develop a strategy for each account where a competitive situation existed. First we met with the account team and found out about the customer: key players, type of IBM equipment, competitive situation, financial analysis, and company goals and objectives.

We had a technology presentation that spoke to each technical aspect of the competitor's product, and why the IBM technology was better. We also had a financial spreadsheet we used to plug in numbers and determine how to cost-justify an IBM system versus the competition.

The most forward-thinking aspect of our approach was to involve third-party leasing companies directly. We worked with them to establish the residual value of the installed equipment and the new IBM equipment. They worked directly with the customer to buy the old equipment, establish a lease on the new equipment, and establish a term for the lease that was quite often a lower rate than their current pricing.

Selby's team was extremely successful in defeating the competition and in selling new IBM equipment. Why? Because of our unique approach and because we used every resource at our disposal to develop and implement our program.

CHAPTER NINETEEN

THE GROUND SHIFTS

Tuesday, Dec. 22

Nick

The doctor said they would have to amputate.

It was the day after my rescue, and he said he thought he could save the balls of my feet, but the toes, at least, would have to go. Probably more.

Large blisters had formed at the top of my feet and he was worried about infection. The doctor explained how muscle could be taken from my stomach and added to my feet to lengthen them after the amputations. That would give me some balance and mobility.

I had been willing to give up my feet if it would save my life, and I would uphold my end of the deal—but only if it was really necessary.

Patricia and I started to look around for other solutions.

Was there a way to save my feet?

Patricia

I started researching and calling around to find out who specialized in frostbite. I wanted to go where the doctors had the most experience with frostbite.

We found treatment centers in Tampa, where we have a home, in Chicago—a city very familiar to us, having lived there for several years—and in San Francisco: the Bunke Clinic. The Bunke Clinic was also highly recommended by one of my husband's business associates.

Then I learned Nick wouldn't be able to fly. Something to do with the pressure in the cabin.

Joyce

Patricia got on the phone. She's a wonder at getting information. She started making telephone calls to find the best doctor for him.

Jennifer

It was definitely an hour-by-hour situation in the beginning. The huge sense of relief we felt when we found he was alive then turned into, "Well, is he going to be okay? What is going to be affected? How will he get around? And work and live a normal life without feet, maybe, or legs?"

At that point we had no idea what the extent of the damage was.

Nick

Patricia enlisted the help of friends and family to search the Internet for experts in frostbite treatment.

After all the research was done, we were told I could not fly. This left us no choice: Only the Bunke Clinic in San Francisco was within ambulance range.

The Tahoe hospital contacted the clinic and made arrangements for the transfer by ambulance.

While all the plans were being made, Patricia began taking over all of my nursing duties other than administering drugs through the IV. She had always been squeamish around hospitals and illness, but this was something she felt she had to do. Somehow, she found the strength to get past her fears, and cared for me better than any nurse could.

I needed the caretaking. Throughout the decisions and preparations, I was high on morphine and other medications. Still, I kept busy answering the many phone calls from friends and relatives, some of whom I hadn't heard from in twenty years.

The wonders of modern technology had made me somewhat of a celebrity. My story had been on NBC national news with Tom Brokaw, and a search of the Internet gave many of the details of my story. I was also giving interviews to any reporter who managed to make it past hospital security.

In one interview, I—in my morphine-induced state—asked for my ski poles and used them as props to describe how I had tried to start a fire. Joyce and Patricia watched this "show" and laughed for the first time in days.

That evening, Roger sat with me while Joyce and Patricia went to get a bite to eat.

Roger

Never, in all that time, even in the wildest imagination, did I imagine Nick was lost somewhere.

You go back and you say, "What would I do differently?"

I was there asleep in the motel room while they were towing his truck away from the ski resort parking lot. I did not have a clue.

You go back and say, "What should I have done?"

Jesse Figueroa

I grew up with Nick. His backyard was catty-corner to mine.

Then I saw his story on the TV news. I called him in the hospital.

When we were kids I'd go stand outside his window and yell "Nicky." Or he'd stand outside mine: "Butchy!" Then off we'd go to some adventure.

We lived in Hubbard, a sleepy village. I remember us trying to find stuff to do. We would get inner tubes and go rafting down the "crick." We used to go fishing in that—we caught a couple of catfish. The steel mill had a dump-off stream, and we used to go skinny-dipping in there. I don't know why we didn't get sick.

In the wintertime we had snowball fights and built snowmen. And every winter, Nick fell in the crick. Once he was running down the embankment and tripped over a log my father would sit on when he went fishing. He went into the ice headfirst that time.

We had about four or five feet of comic books apiece, and we'd take them over to each other's house and just read 'em all.

We used to pretend we were brothers, and even gave ourselves a big last name: Dante. We thought we could impress the girls.

I remember Nick was always on restriction for something. I would hear his mom, "Nicholas Joseph!" and wonder, "Oh-oh, what'd he do now?"

We'd walk on the ice to cross the crick. We'd hear cracking, then jump down and spread out.

Then one of us got the idea—probably Nick—to see how big of a snowball we could make and roll off the dam. Nick went first, but the edge broke and he fell in. He went totally under, only his hands were showing. But he swam up, grabbed the board, and walked across the dam anyway. We ran across to my house to dry off so his mom wouldn't know. It was about a mile away. She knew anyway.

Thomas Blanchard
Salomon Smith Barney

I got a call from a client of mine who had seen Nick on TV. They had interviewed him in his hospital bed.

The only reason this client knew Nick was also a client of mine is because we did some insurance work together for Nick and Patricia. He had spoken with Nick, and we were putting together a proposal for Nick. Life insurance.

That's how I found out he was still alive.

Dr. Greg Bunke
Bunke Clinic
San Francisco

My dad is really the pioneer of this field. He's considered "the father of micro-surgery."

He did this starting in the late 1950s to early '60s. The concept of being able to repair blood vessels under the microscope so you could transplant tissue—that was the whole idea.

Before then, if somebody had amputated part of their body, you couldn't put it back on. The blood vessels were so small.

Over about a ten-year period—doing a lot of the research actually at our house, in our garage—he did the first toe-to-hand transplant. It was done on a Rhesus monkey in our garage when I was probably eight or ten years old. My mom helped him. She's a dermatologist and was his first assistant.

Then, after the first tests, it was done in the laboratory.

Once we knew we could do that, then fingers were put back on. He did the first toe-to-thumb transplant. He did the first "replantation" of an entire scalp (it had been torn off somebody). He started teaching people how to do it. He's helped create microsurgery labs and services around the world.

That's what we're doing in San Francisco. I trained with him in the 1980s and then joined his practice in 1987.

That's basically what we do all day: either "replantation," which is putting stuff back on, or "transplantation," which is taking parts from one part of the body and transplanting them to another part of the body.

Linda

My phone rang the next day, the day after they found Nick. "Linda, it's Nick."

I said, "Oh my gosh, Nick!"

He said, "The first thing I wanted to say was thank you for all your help and persistence."

I said, "Oh, yeah, absolutely. Team effort. There were three of us looking for you." I couldn't have done it without the help of other people.

I'm glad it was a success story and not… the other.

Commitment:

A Good Team Needs It

Even though I was out of touch because of my medications, my team took care of me. They were committed to working together to find and execute the best solutions.

This is also the kind of commitment it takes to start a company.

Ray Lin and Boris Auerbach founded Premisys in Silicon Valley in 1993. It was the first company in the telecommunications industry to focus on several solutions at once: voice, data, and video. It was a big challenge.

There were many times when both Boris and Ray worked entire days and nights. Ray was CEO, COO, and CFO, as well as manager of production, accounting, human resources, and lead sales person. Boris was CTO, VP engineering, and head of procurement, marketing, and product design.

And somehow, they even kept some balance with their family lives.

The hard work and commitment paid off. When they finally got financed, they received a multi-million dollar first round investment—a large amount at the time. The company became the premier provider of integrated access solutions, went public, and at one point had a market cap approaching $1 billion.

CHAPTER TWENTY

THE BEGINNING, THE END

Wednesday, Dec. 23

Nick

On December 23, I was finally stable enough to make the trip to San Francisco.

I was loaded into the ambulance with my foot tent and a four-hour supply of morphine. Joyce drove Patricia—in the car I had driven up to Tahoe.

The tow company had delivered it to the hospital for us. Roger had arranged this. As usual, he was covering bases none of us thought of. Roger and Patricia had been working as a team for the past few days, and it was hard for her to see him go. But by then, he had a nasty cold; he also needed to get to Colorado to spend the holidays with his own family.

Patricia and Joyce followed the ambulance all the way into San Francisco, and we arrived at the hospital around 4:00 p.m. The staff met us and escorted us to a private room.

Dr. Bunke then explained his ideas for treating my frostbite.

The major goal was to save as much of each foot as possible. Patricia and I were willing to do anything to achieve this goal.

Dr. Bunke

I think he probably should have died.

That amount of exposure, for that amount of time—your body temperature drops to a point where, physiologically, things just don't work. Your heart stops working.

Somehow he was able to maintain his body temperature to a point things kept circulating.

The problems with exposed parts getting frozen—I'm surprised his hands didn't get it. Ears, nose, lips—they can often get pretty badly damaged. That's usually what we see. It's usually more. Especially with the degree of damage he had to his feet.

His feet had gotten wet. That could be one of the explanations for why his feet got significantly worse than the rest of his body.

Nick

The first course of action was to do a sonogram of the feet to determine the extent of blood flow. This test revealed there was indeed some blood flow in the feet and even in some toes. It was decided my feet would have to be continually elevated above my heart to promote optimum blood flow. I would also take blood thinners. When there was no further sign of healthy tissue growth, then he would amputate whatever was necessary.

We were told this could take six weeks or longer. We resigned ourselves to it. But just as we were getting settled into a beautiful and spacious hospital room, the nurses announced I was being moved to the intensive care unit—the ICU.

I would be treated like a heart patient with a nitroglycerin drip for the next forty-eight hours.

We would now be spending Christmas in the ICU.

Resourcefulness:

Make it Work

When I was CEO at Premisys, I had the opportunity to work with Claude Dupuis, VP of Engineering.

We asked Claude to put together a development team for one of our new products. Claude started in October, before even moving to our base in San Francisco—he worked out of his home in Ottawa. By January he had thirty engineers working for him and had a development lab set up in Canada.

From the very beginning we could count on Claude to get the job done on time and within budget. He had a unique way of motivating people and making sure they were held accountable for their delivery schedules. His approach was to be there with his people during crunch time—when the engineers worked many hours to complete a product development effort so the product would be on schedule.

When he became VP of Engineering, he led the Canadian and U.S. development teams, about eighty people in all. He worked very closely with Marketing and Sales to be sure products were being developed with the right feature sets. He also could be relied upon to call on customers to explain the technical aspects of the products, and to glean from the customers all he could about their requirements.

But Claude's resourcefulness and persistence really set him apart. He set up a way of tracking development projects that showed very clearly the status of each product and every feature. This development schedule became our "bible" when quoting development time frames to customers and Wall Street analysts.

When a schedule was in jeopardy of slipping, Claude's persistence and tenacity kicked in. He would work very closely with the engineers involved in a project and determine how to get it back on track, knowing slippage in a development schedule is very costly. With Claude in charge, we rarely missed our target dates.

Claude became a key player as we became involved in trying to sell Premisys. He clearly described the architecture and design of our products to potential buyers. He also was very good at getting the right people involved at the right time—whatever it took to make things work.

CHAPTER TWENTY-ONE

ROUND TWO

Christmas week

Nick

Thankfully I was the only patient on the floor that Christmas Eve. The rules were very relaxed and Patricia was able to stay in the room with me—she even managed to climb into the hospital bed with me. We watched television all day and the nurses shared their eggnog with us. Patricia had made arrangements for our children to fly into San Francisco that evening.

Nickie and Jennifer arrived at the stroke of midnight.

We were once again a family. Suddenly, anything seemed possible now that we had each other. We were determined to make this holiday as normal as possible.

Luckily, our San Francisco home was only ten minutes from the hospital. Patricia took the kids home, got them settled in, and spent the first night in a long time in her own bed.

Patricia

The kids walked into the hospital room just after midnight, just to say "hi" to their dad Christmas morning.

Later in the day my best friend Joyce brought Christmas dinner. We actually had quite a few people in the ICU. We were able to do that because there were no other patients, so they were very liberal with us.

Joyce

It was my boyfriend's idea. The kids flew in on Christmas Eve from Florida. We were talking, and we knew they were going to be there at the hospital, all alone, and Bob said, "You know what, why don't we just bring them Christmas dinner?" The supermarkets here, they make holiday dinners you can order and pick up.

We got the very last one. We had to beg them to put one more in, but they did. We brought some homemade stuff, too, and we brought them Christmas dinner, which was really nice, because it was pretty dismal in the hospital.

Jennifer

Eventually, I did end up going to Florida. Nickie, my brother, and I flew out together to San Francisco. By that time we knew my father was in the hospital in San Francisco. We visited him

Christmas Eve; we got in rather late. Then we spent Christmas in the hospital with my father.

He had his Christmas shopping done. He gave my brother a ring.

He gave me a little Limoges box with a cat on top and a little pin inside, which I keep next to my bed. That was quite amazing he actually had time to buy us Christmas presents. It's something I keep with me as a memory, as a reminder there's hope, always.

It was a Christmas miracle.

Nick, Jr.

It was difficult.

We spent Christmas in the hospital. We opened all our gifts in the Intensive Care unit. We exchanged cards. All of us were there, friends came in. I think we even ate dinner in there. We did.

My father gave me a gold ring he picked out that year for me, prior to all this happening. I guess he was going to give me that, so it's something I always keep right here. That would have been the last thing he gave me. Instead of it being the last thing he gave me, it was something he was planning on giving me, so I have it.

It was pretty symbolic.

We just took turns in the hospital. We all hung out there, and all watched football with him. We prayed for the best, and, considering the alternative, I think we got the best.

Nick

The children had managed to squeeze quite a few presents into their luggage, and we had the unique experience of having Christmas dinner in an ICU room. Joyce and her family provided the traditional meal and we were joined by our good friends Mardi and Rick. At one point, we had eleven people in a very small room.

We all agreed being together was the best Christmas present we could have wished for.

Nick, Jr.

I had to get back to dental school in New York. That was just after my first semester of dental school. It was a lot of stress, constantly calling back and forth, back and forth, to see how my dad was doing. And I had moved to a new city, living in a big city in a new place—it was tough.

Nick

It was a relief to be moved back into a normal room the next day. We could finally get into a routine. Patricia performed nursing duties. The nurses had pretty much given her free rein on the floor.

Once the children left to go home, Patricia and I settled into a routine. She arrived every morning at seven with breakfast and a Starbucks coffee. She would then bathe me and change my bed using linens from home. The nurses loved her—they never had to come into the room. Patricia would walk out into the Castro district around the corner from the hospital to get us lunch. In the afternoon, she walked home, prepared dinner, and came back to the hospital by 5:00. Her day ended around 11:00 p.m.

She was an amazing caregiver. I will be forever thankful for her persistence, love and kindness during this difficult period for both of us.

During this time, I attempted to conduct business with Premisys.

The morphine was a problem, however. I couldn't think clearly.

At one point, I talked with several Premisys executives and decided to step down as CEO. However, after some discussion with Patricia, I decided I had made a mistake. I stayed on as CEO.

During one of our lazy afternoons in the hospital, the staff psychiatrist paid us a visit. He told us he was working with Dr. Bunke and wanted to discuss the trauma of my ordeal and possible repercussions, such as nightmares.

I insisted there was no trauma associated with my experience—certainly no nightmares—and promptly fell asleep. Meanwhile, he kept rambling on.

Later, we received a bill for $250 for his "service." Patricia paid the bill and released some pent-up anxiety in an accompanying, scathing letter, so perhaps it was worth something.

This was one of the few times during the entire period of my care we were not completely satisfied with the professionalism of the staff.

Dr. Bunke

We did bone scans on Nick. You inject some fluid in the vein that has material to "tag" bone that is alive. You're put into a machine that can sense where this material is. If his toes were not viable, then they wouldn't light up.

That was a way to predict what would be alive—to predict what could be saved.

Nick

By the new year, the blisters on my feet grew to the size of small balloons. The hospital staff tried to keep them intact as long as possible. Once they broke, the chance for infection was tremendous.

I was told home care was not only a possibility but was preferable to hospital care: there are fewer germs at home than in the hospital.

Joyce

Going home—that was another experience. The Williams house was a three-story Victorian, and all the bedrooms were on the third floor. There was no way we were going to be able to get him up the stairs.

Patricia made arrangements for a hospital bed, and the day before he was to come home from the hospital, my sons and I went over to the house. We moved all of the furniture out of the ground floor family room, and got the bed set up.

When he did come home, they were able to just take him straight into the downstairs room.

I bought him one of those clappers for his lights. Then, we knew if Patricia was on the second or third floor, and he needed her, she wouldn't hear him by yelling. So my oldest son went and got some walkie-talkies.

Nick

The hospital bed was delivered, complete with air circulator to prevent bedsores. Patricia managed to find a wheelchair with leg elevators, and had a set of wheelchair ramps installed on the first floor.

I still had to get there.

Before I could come home I had to wean myself from the morphine. My desire to get home was so strong I did this in just two days, switching to Vicodin. While I was switching from morphine to Vicodin, the blisters on my feet finally broke. The nurses showed Patricia how to clean and bandage my feet. Twice daily my feet were bathed in a saline solution and then covered in a thick white cream. It looked like Crisco. My feet were then wrapped in gauze. All of the skin had to be covered.

After the instructions, the nurses gave Patricia bags of bandages and ointment and sent us on our way home.

Tony Flores

I was VP of operations while Nick was CEO at Premisys.

There was some serious concern from a business standpoint. But Nick was able to stay on as CEO.

A lot of that had to do with his personality. He always maintained that positive, upbeat attitude—it certainly was a reflection on his ability to manage not only himself, but also the company.

First of all, and I've always told him this, he's the one person I know who always seems to really have that kind of attitude. I've never met anybody like this—always positive, upbeat, and forward-looking.

Myself, I'd be fairly depressed in his situation. But he never even thought for one minute this was going to be anything. He continued to move forward, he continued to exercise, he continued to run—he continued to go to Lake Tahoe.

He just kept up that attitude of his. I think in a lot of ways it contributes to his success.

The mere fact he wanted to stand when he came back for the company meeting—it was something. I remember his perseverance in wanting to make that happen.

To this day I'm always amazed at his ability to think fast. He always had enough information to make a decision. That's the way it should be done.

That's what made him a great guy and a great CEO.

Nick

We had a company-wide meeting while I was still in the hospital. I was on the conference phone. I spoke a little bit; I didn't speak long, because I was on morphine.

I made a commitment to the company I would come back on February 9—less than two months away—for the next company meeting—and I would stand in front of people and be there.

As it turned out, I hadn't yet had the surgery on my feet.

But I could stand, and I did. I stood, I leaned against a table, and I talked to everybody about what I had been through.

I related it to what was required for our company to be successful. People listened.

It is so important to always pick out the positive aspects of a situation—especially when you are the leader, out in front of the people in the company.

You, in your job, and I, as CEO of my company, are the leaders.

Your people are looking to you for positive inspiration—not negativism, ever.

And they're looking for decisions.

There's nothing worse than NOT making a decision, especially when it applies to people, and the company.

They're looking for the leadership of the company—not just the CEO, but others—to make a decision based on information they have, whether it's about products, customers, whatever.

You can't just let it linger.

Ed Thompson
VP of Manufacturing, Paradyne

I've skied with Nick before. I've also run with Nick.

He did a half-marathon with me, which was probably somewhat above his capability at the time. But he just reached down into...something, and brought out what he needed to do that.

I knew, when I heard about this, if anybody could pull this off, Nick could do it. I've always been impressed with Nick's ability to make things happen and be resourceful.

Teamwork:

Work Together to Win

When I worked for Tellabs Corp., we acquired Martis, located in Espoo, Finland. It was an outstanding company.

The founder, Timo Lefthonen, was an accountant by trade but taught himself electrical engineering by reading textbooks. He went on to design high-speed modems and a network management system, then added more products.

We acquired Martis in October of 1993. At that time, Timo was the CEO—and was also the VP Sales, CFO, controller, and VP engineering. In short, he did all the executive functions in the company except manufacturing.

That was done by his brother.

The product line was the best in the industry. Martis had managed to sell to Telecom Finland, the Swedish telephone company, and most other Scandinavian telco's. The revenues the year we acquired Martis were $40 million and the company was accretive to Tellabs' bottom line immediately. In the next three years Martis revenues were $80, $120, and $200 million, respectively. The revenues increased each year as we began to sell the product outside of Scandinavia, first into Western Europe and then into Latin America and Asia Pacific.

In 1994, the Finns from the manufacturing department of Martis visited Tellabs.

The trip lasted four days. The last day was St. Patrick's Day. That day, I was called to take the Finns into Chicago. I took all six to our condo for lunch with Patricia. It was a gorgeous day in Chicago and the view from our 30th-floor condo was spectacular.

Nonetheless, the Finns had very little to say. We couldn't tell whether it was shyness or lack of English. After lunch, we started walking; Patricia would meet us downtown later.

In case you don't know, Chicago pretty much closes down for the afternoon of St. Patty's Day. There is a big parade, and the river is dyed green.

The Finns and I began our celebration at Lizzy McNiel's, an Irish pub—even the beer was green—and then on to the famous Billy Goat Bar. The Finns thoroughly enjoyed both places and began to open up.

Their English, in fact, was very good.

We talked about how to be successful together and many other things.

By the end of the night, the Finns were a group of very open, very friendly people. And fun: I took a picture of the Finns standing in a row with Patricia laying flat across their outstretched arms.

We had become friends and I had good contacts at Martis whenever I needed a special favor.

Never pass up an opportunity for teamwork, no matter the situation.

CHAPTER TWENTY-TWO

THE CLIMB

January

Nick

My feet looked like they had been put through a meat grinder. Felt like it, too.

Every time Patricia cleaned and bandaged them, the pain was intense. When the old bandages were removed, it felt like someone was ripping the skin from the tops of my feet. There were open wounds where the blisters had been. I had to steel myself before the saline solution was applied. The burning sensation brought tears to my eyes.

When Patricia got out the jar of Silverdene cream and applied it to the tops of my feet, the feeling of relief was overwhelming. I could now relax until the next dreaded treatment. Rarely did I allow anyone to watch this procedure because I did not want anyone to see me cry. This was something I could only share with my wife.

One time a business associate was visiting and wanted to stay while the feet were being bandaged. He had a hard time taking no for an answer. It is strange, but I think he wanted to use my feet as a topic of gossip. My brother David and my wife finally had to force this so-called friend to leave.

Once home, we settled into a routine that worked for both of us—though Patricia hadn't realized how challenging and demanding nursing would be. Worse, we lived in a Victorian home with three flights of stairs. She ran up and down many times each day.

Her days were filled with caring for my feet, bathing me, preparing meals for me, and helping me move when necessary.

Joyce

I went to the Williams home every weekend.

Usually on Friday I would take BART (Bay Area Rapid Transit) over and stay until Sunday and then just take the BART back.

You do what you can, when you can.

It was all through the winter. It was rainy and cold and windy. Nick was totally bedridden for all those weeks before he got in the wheelchair. His feet had to stay elevated.

He had to go back and forth to the clinic. It was really a hard time. It was an exhausting time.

If one of their friends or Nick's brother was there, then Patricia and I would go to the movies for a couple of hours, or just take a walk—just to get her out. She couldn't really leave the house at all—he was totally helpless. If anything happened, he would not have been able to do anything. If she went out to one of the little corner stores nearby, she had to take her phone.

You have no idea how many steps were in this house. It's three stories, but these Victorian three-stories—the steps are straight up. You're running up and down the stairs constantly.

She never complained. She'd say she was tired, but that was as far as it went. She was just tired.

It was a long haul.

It was a lot of teamwork. They both followed what they were supposed to do to a T, which I'm sure expedited his recovery and his healing process. It really boiled down to the two of them, working together, to speed his recovery.

Maryann

There was a hospital bed, and it dwarfed the room. The room wasn't that large. You just had a little bit of space on either side.

Yet, it didn't feel like a hospital room. It didn't feel like a sick person's room. It felt like the hub of something.

I don't know if they noticed that.

I think it was a wonderful thing. The vitality, the strength and determination—of both Nick and Patricia.

It didn't feel like chicken broth and fevers, that kind of thing.

I think it was different than you and me being sick. It didn't feel like "sick."

They really are two strong individuals.

Nick

At times we felt we were prisoners in our own home. The wheelchair ramps were a godsend. It was exhilarating to get fresh air and feel the sun on my face. I realized how lucky I was to be alive.

My friends and my brother David visited and helped to get

me outdoors. Rick came almost every weekend, muscled me into my wheel chair, up the ramp and pushed me around the streets of San Francisco. He even took me for rides in my Porsche—a job he really hated.

He even volunteered to drive me every day, if necessary.

Maryann

Their house was probably the worst situation for anybody with anything wrong with a limb. If you came in from the garage, there were two steps to go up to the hall. If you came in the front door, you had to go down two steps to the family room, which became Nick's room.

While I was there, a friend of Nick's came over. We took Nick on his first walk. This guy was very, very strong.

Of course, San Francisco is not the best place to have a wheelchair. You're going up and down hills. My job was running ahead to make sure nobody bumped into his foot. His legs couldn't be down—they had to be out straight.

We went to a church that first day. Nick had promised God something. I don't know what it was. But he wanted to go in that church. So this friend pushed and I ran interference, and we went to a church a couple of blocks away. He wanted to fulfill a promise he had made on the mountain.

Jennifer

Sometime around the Super Bowl I was in San Francisco for one of my father's surgeries. I remember it was then because we took my father to a friend's house for the Super Bowl in a wheel-chair. I think it was the first time he had been out socially.

Nick

Al Siders, a good friend from Chicago, came one weekend and pushed me around the neighborhood. We took a road trip to enjoy the beautiful San Francisco scenery and climate, and even stopped for drinks in one of the local saloons.

We were creative in devising ways to keep my feet above my heart at all times. We used foam rubber wedges in my bed, the wheel chair, and in the car.

Patricia took me out in the wheelchair, too, but she was more selective about our route because of the hills.

On our walks, we faced struggles disabled people face every day.

Most people would not give way to the wheelchair on the side-walk.

Once while crossing the street with the walk sign, a man in a car making a right turn almost hit us. He didn't want to wait for us to cross. Patricia screamed at him and he stopped the car but refused to get out. I think he saw her murderous glare and was truly afraid of my wife.

We had restaurants refuse to seat us because they did not want to accommodate a wheelchair. Sometimes a reminder of federal laws for the disabled quickly got us a table.

Neither Patricia nor I were afraid to speak up. These outings were so important to us. We needed to get away from our home hospital.

Maryann

When he had to go to the office, that was also a challenge. He would hire a car to drive him, but it had to be deep enough so his legs could stick out straight.

Plus, the hill in front of the house was steep. Even getting in and out of the car was a challenge. And the traffic—it's a major road.

It just was a logistic nightmare to do just about anything.

Nick

I looked forward to the many calls, gifts, letters, and cards that arrived daily.

One call came from a friend I had not seen since grade school. Another came from a Korean War frostbite victim who told me his story and gave words of encouragement. One day an envelope came filled with letters and drawings from a third grade Sunday school class. My favorite was from "Paul"; he thought I was very brave but reminded me to bring my compass next time.

Another time, a friend came bearing gifts including a bottle of Opus One wine—one of my favorites. Since I could not drink, I asked my friends to drink it for me and tell me how good it was. They gladly complied.

My lack of physical exercise was worrisome.

With the help of a good friend, Kristin Rostek, a training regimen was set up. Kristin has a degree in personal training and is a licensed massage therapist. Three times a week she put me through my paces. I did weight training, stretching, sit-ups and leg exercises, all while laying in my bed with my feet elevated. These sessions helped me physically and mentally.

Maryann

Nick worked out. He had a personal trainer come in. It was smart, I think, because I think it was so boring and tedious being in that bed.

Then he would be drenched with sweat. It took so much energy, to deal with the pain and healing, and then on top of that, he was pushing himself.

I think that was very healthy of him.

He had tons of company. Lots of times, it was work people who would come and have meetings. Sometimes it was doctors, and then of course friends.

I don't think there was a day there weren't people there.

It was a very, very busy place.

Nick, Jr.

My uncle flew out to help for a long time; he had some friends out there.

My mother, of course, who basically—well, without her, I don't know how my father would have made it. She pretty much did everything for him those couple of months.

She brought him back to life.

Roger

We were both living in San Francisco. I walked him in his wheelchair. One time we went to Chinese New Year downtown, with him in his wheelchair, his feet sticking up in the air.

Patricia

I have a good network of friends. I'm blessed.

Joyce and Bob spent that entire week, entire days at Tahoe with him, with me, and she was there *every* weekend to help me care for him.

Maryann came out for a whole week to help me care for him. My friend Peg came out for a whole week to help me care for him.

Those are the important people. People who gave their time, who loved us both enough to come and help. That's what I needed. I needed the help.

They were doing menial things, but it meant so much to me. They gave me a chance just to focus on Nick. They cooked, and they cleaned, and they did the laundry. It doesn't sound like much, but believe me. It was. They are people who sat on the phone and listened to me cry and carry on, and spent all that time helping me focus so I could go back downstairs and continue. I couldn't have done it without them.

Maryann

I went out there later. It was early on; they hadn't done any of the amputation yet. They were waiting to see. Sometime, I guess, skin can surprise you. They didn't know how much he might recover. I cannot even imagine the pain he was in. He didn't complain.

Nick always teases me. Everyone teases me. Apparently I'm an easy mark. You know how people always want to show you their incisions? When Patricia was changing his bandages, he wanted me to look. And there was no way on this earth I was going to.

I could tell it was killing him. I could see it in his face. That was almost too painful, to see his face.

He would just perspire. He'd be drenched. And you could tell from his face.

But truthfully? He still laughed. We laughed a lot.

Thomas Blanchard
Salomon Smith Barney

Two to four weeks later I spoke with Nick. We talked about it, and he explained the whole story to me.

I'll never forget the one comment I asked him. I said, "Nick, do you mind if I ask—are you a very religious guy? Do you believe in God?" He goes, "Absolutely."

I asked if that helped. He says on the second day, when things were looking pretty grim, he said, "Well, God, I'm not going down without a fight. If this is how you're going to take me, I'm not going to go easy, because I want to see my wife and children again."

I can only imagine what keeps you going at that point, when you think death is near and no one's going to find you and you're freezing to death. It's just amazing.

Obviously, with his training in the Marine Corps, he had survival skills, and I'm sure that helped too. But it's just amazing.

Nick

Trying to run a company from a home hospital bed was a challenge.

But my company helped me. We set up a high-speed phone line and tied me into the company telephone system, complete with my company number and extension. The equipment also allowed me to connect into the company LAN for email and Internet access. This turned out to be a very effective way for me to maintain contact and keep up-to-date on all necessary issues. I continued to attend all scheduled meetings via conference call.

After two weeks in this mode, I decided I had to go in to the office. A Board of Directors meeting had been scheduled to make several important decisions—including whether or not I should remain as CEO. My presence was essential.

Getting into a suit and tie was no easy task. Patricia had to carefully guide my feet through the pant legs. They were very sore and even the slightest touch felt like a knife-stick.

After getting dressed, a limo picked me up and brought me to the office. Patricia went along to help with all the personal tasks I couldn't handle by myself.

The meeting went without a hitch. I remained CEO. We

decided I could continue to conduct most business from home; I would travel to the office two days each week using the car service.

Resourcefulness:

Use Your Team to Succeed Despite Change

Our company had a big opportunity in Japan. But could we pull it off?

Paradyne, like many other telecommunication equipment companies, was dramatically affected by a slowdown in the telecommunications industry around 2000. As a result, they reduced headcount in many areas—especially manufacturing, since production requirements were significantly reduced.

Then, late in 2001, the sales team uncovered an opportunity for a big sale of one of our advanced products, modems, in Japan. One catch: 250,000 units would have to be up and running in only six months. And we hadn't even made them yet.

Ed Thompson, our VP of Operations, developed a plan with his team.

"We had to go out and rent a lot of equipment, and we had to do it very, very quickly," says Ed. "We had to bring in some temporary labor, almost twice as many as we had permanent workers already in the plant."

He was scheduled to go on vacation in the Azores for a week. He canceled.

"My wife went on without me," he says. "She sent me a postcard."

He would have to not only build the product quickly, but test it.

"We were sending the product to Japan," he says, "and their quality standards are high."

It would require a production line about 500 feet long.

"Probably about 12 different large pieces over the 500 feet," says Ed, including both assembly and testing.

"We didn't know before where we would rent the equipment. We searched far and wide. Finally, after a pretty exhaustive search, we found the factory that made the equipment—and they had some we could rent," he says.

"It got a little dicey. Time was passing, and we hadn't gotten the equipment rented. We were getting a little bit nervous."

Finally, they found it.

"We brought it in quickly," he says. "We had known it would be possible to rent equipment—we just didn't know where."

Next: Assembling the assembly line.

"We had space already," he says. "We cleared out some equipment that was already in the area. We had some riggers, because it is very heavy equipment normal people couldn't move safely. The riggers come in, jockey the equipment into place. We had the factory reps out to make sure the equipment was set up and running okay."

They were able to get it in, get it up and running, bring in the people, train them, and get them running.

The product started at one end as components; the other end it came off in "D" containers.

"A 'D' container," says Ed, "is basically a huge

cardboard box that had in it 100 of these modems, each of which were in their own individual box, with cables and manuals and power cords."

The company already had two lines up and running in the regular plant, but they were running at maybe half capacity, he says.

"This work required us to use the third line we installed, all three shifts, and of course the other two lines, all three shifts," says Ed. "So it was running essentially around the clock."

Meanwhile, the customer assumed everything was business as usual.

"That's the way it works," says Ed. "You dive into that empty swimming pool and hope it fills up."

But it was a no-fail situation, he says.

"This brought in a great deal of cash for the company," says Ed. "I think a lot of people would have just gone to an outsource: 'Here—someone else do it.' But we knew if we did it here, we could do it very cheap. The incremental cost to do it here would be very small, even though you had to rent the equipment."

Because it ramped up, and then had a finite end to it, he believed the company could do it and then ramp it down very quickly.

"We knew we had control of the situation and that we could do a good job," says Ed. "We've dealt with outsourcing before, and some of them are good, but you can have problems dealing with people remotely."

Because they were temporary people, they could be let go at the end without any problem, and because the equipment was rented, it could be sent back.

"So, that expense that would normally continue did not continue," says Ed. "It was a good deal for us, and we were able to get the work done without the expense drain continuing."

The result: The customer order was filled completely and on time, and the company received over $500,000 in revenue.

Many people would have said this was an impossible task. Not Ed.

He accepted the challenge, brought in his team, was creative and resourceful, and succeeded.

CHAPTER TWENTY-THREE

PAIN AND LOSS

Febrary

Nick

As the weeks passed, my feet, suspended in mid-air, improved. Dr. Bunke checked me every week. But the day came when the improvement was over.

It was time to amputate.

I was admitted back into the hospital in February, 1999. The first surgery was to remove my toes. I was in good spirits, thanking God that only toes had to be amputated, not my feet.

Within hours of the first surgery, my feet were unwrapped for inspection.

Patricia

I made sure I was there when they unbandaged his feet. I didn't want him to see them.

When they amputated, I knew this was going to be so painful for him. He had six pops of morphine and it still didn't touch the pain. When they unbandaged his feet, they looked like they had been through a meat grinder.

How I sat on the edge of his bed and held his hand and looked at those feet without passing out, to this day I'll never know.

"You know, they're really not that bad, Nick," I said to him. "I think, with skin grafts, they'll be fine." I convinced him of that.

He did peek at them and then immediately looked away and would not look again until they put the grafts on.

How do you convey that? How do you even write those emotions down?

Nick

I nearly passed out as I looked at what was left.

Large chunks of my feet had been removed where my big toes had been. Four other toes were also gone. There was no skin in the area where my toes had been; I could see bone. Patricia was with me as they uncovered my feet. I turned my head and she held me as Dr. Bunke and his surgical team did their inspection.

After this, my feet healed for a day. Then I went back for a second surgery.

A ten-by-three-inch patch of skin was removed from my thigh and used to cover the wounds on my feet. Then I had two weeks of recovery in the hospital. I was given morphine to handle the pain. Once again, in order to go home, I had to get myself off morphine. I was able to deal with the pain fairly well, switched to Vicodin, and was released to go home.

Back home, I once again used the hospital bed in our family

room and was hooked up to work as before. I attended most meetings via conference phone and two days per week was at the office in person.

Dr. Bunke said I no longer needed a wheelchair, and I used crutches to get around for about a week. I wondered if I would ever walk normally again without toes. My physical therapist said I would eventually be able to do everything as I once had. The therapy was slow at first.

The first time I stood without crutches, I nearly passed out from the pain. Within one week, however, I was down to one crutch, and by the following week I was using a cane.

The cane lasted another week. By early April, I was walking on my own.

Dr. Bunke

I've been up to the same slopes skiing a couple of times, and think of Nick frequently—especially on a windy day.

But people get stuck out there a lot. It happens relatively frequently. Most people don't make it.

Nick

Do I blame others for not finding me sooner?

No. Nah. It was my fault, you know? I should have told people what I was doing. That didn't happen, and they didn't find me. That was my problem. I have no hard feelings about that. Not a problem.

Roger

I've thought about it a lot since then.

You think about "what if?" What if we hadn't acted right away? What if we had waited another day? What if we hadn't realized he was gone?

Or this: What if we had acted sooner, or tried different things? How many more toes would he have? How much less pain would he have?

Those are the kind of things you think about.

What if?

Claude Dupuis

It's hard to say what would have happened if we had gone skiing with Nick that weekend after all.

We've been skiing since then. We went back to Squaw.

Maryann

Nick was a Marine *before* he was a Marine. That expectation would be there that he would *have* to survive. He would be so disappointed in himself if he didn't.

He tells his story all the time. It reminds me of the "Rime of the Ancient Mariner," where the Ancient Mariner absolutely *has* to tell his story, he *needs* to tell his story.

I know it was hard for Patricia to hear it over and over again.

To her it was fear, and pain; she had had no control over the situation.

But for Nick, I think it was how he came to terms with it. He had to tell his story.

CHAPTER TWENTY-FOUR

UPHILL

Spring

Patricia

We went to our home in Florida for Easter. Nick's feet were still bandaged; they were still bleeding.

We had to get the bulkhead seat in the airplane because his feet still had to be propped up. I got a wheelchair to use at the airport. He still wasn't back to full speed by any stretch of the imagination.

Nick, Jr.

I had to stay in New York for dental school, so the next time I saw my father was in Florida. The same place. It was Easter. He was already there.

I flew in late. I woke up in the morning and my dad was in the kitchen—standing. Walking around, with his feet all

169

bandaged up. He probably shouldn't have been standing, but it was just the way he is. He wanted to appear probably better than he was to me. Either way, next time I saw him he was up, standing.

It was a big surprise to see him walking around. I was glad ~~that~~ he could at least get around again.

I was busy with school, but we still kept in touch constantly.

Jennifer

He was always active and exercising and running even from my earliest memories. I'm sure being in shape had a lot to do with it.

He managed to stay active—even without toes. Nothing was stopping him. He went running, and then ended up with fractures in his feet because he was running.

That's my father.

Nothing will keep him down.

Nick

My feet continued to bleed. Patricia and I traveled to our home in Florida in late April. The warm weather and the beach were a very welcome break after the surgeries and therapy. I was self-conscious about my feet. I kept them covered with white socks as we sat around the pool and when I went swimming.

When we returned from Florida, Dr. Bunke continued to examine my feet periodically until July. The bleeding continued until October, but I was told I could do everything. I began my normal running and workout regime in May. It was painful, but it made me feel almost back to normal.

Dr. Bunke

Nick was very inspiring. He was the guy who was going to get better no matter what.

All we can do is put the anatomy back together as close to normal as possible. If the patients have the right attitude, they flourish—they take off. It's the ones who don't do that who sink into this horrible depressive abyss.

We have what we call the "super-survivor club." They're patients who have had horrible, devastating injuries: arms torn off, big facial burns.

Some of them do better than I know I could ever do. They're the ones who go on with the rest of their lives and do incredibly well. They actually do better—I think *physically* do better. Something happens, something in the way the body physiology works.

If you're thinking positively, there's something about how your body heals. It's something we have no understanding of, but we've seen it.

The "super-survivors"—it's an informal group. Whenever we see them we say, "Oh, he's part of our 'super-survivor club.'"

No doubt. Nick's in that group.

EPILOGUE

Nick

When I returned to work, I decided to tell my story to the people in my company. I hoped it would provide them with some inspiration and perspective.

The first time was very difficult.

I have continued to tell my story, and to talk about the attributes that helped me survive—commitment, positive attitude, resourcefulness, teamwork, and perseverance—and have helped me in my professional life.

I believe these attributes can help you, too.

They can set you apart from others in any organization, and help you with life situations.

Taking these attributes to heart can help make each of us as successful as we want to be.

Acknowledgments

First to be thanked—for never giving up on me, and for the great detective work that led to my rescue—my dear Patricia, my good friend Roger Dorf, and my assistant at the time, Linda McFarland.

Thank you to the staff at Lake Tahoe Forest Hospital for excellent care and for dealing with the press. A special thanks to Dr. Greg Bunke and his staff and all the staff at California Pacific Medical Center for excellent medical care.

For their support throughout my ordeal: my daughter Jennifer, my son Nicholas, and my brother David. Thank you to my good friends Joyce Canzionieri, Bob Coonradt, Roger Dorf, Kristen Rostek, Al Siders, Peg Lawrence, Maryann Schoulz, Rick and Mardi Drew, David Hallman and Kim Binder, who graciously and lovingly took time out of their busy lives to help Patricia care for me.

And thank you again to Patricia for her kind and gentle care and persistence.

For endless cards and calls, thank you to many friends and relatives too numerous to mention.

And the ultimate thanks to God for saving me.

APPENDIX ONE

POSTSCRIPT

Galeen Stratton
Dependable Tow
Tahoe

Nowadays, when cars get towed from the ski resort parking lots, they're checking on the owners. They check on that real strenuously.

A lot of times, especially if there's been new snow, they'll call and say, "Did any of the cars not get picked up?"

Or if we've got a car that hasn't been picked up, and nobody's contacted us, we're calling them and saying, "Hey, are you sure you don't have anybody missing on the mountain?"

When we do private properties, they all get reported to the highway patrol so the license plate number goes into the highway patrol computer.

Roger Dorf

If I had the experience again, I would assume there was something wrong, and think earlier, faster.

For people in a ski area, if there is someone missing, the first thing you do is call the Sheriff's department and see if there's some kind of record of their car having been towed.

The natural things you think of are, "Was there an accident? Are they in the hospital?" I thought this. But I didn't think he was lost. That was the last thing in my mind. I was assuming he was with two other people.

There are little cues you can learn from this:

Don't rationalize. Assume something went wrong.

Don't give up until you track it down and find out otherwise.

Don't assume everything is okay. Most people would tend to assume everything is okay in a situation like this. But maybe it isn't.

Jennifer Williams

I think I look at things maybe a little more optimistically if I'm going through a bad time. Right now my fiancé is deployed with the military. Through the whole thing, I've just been rather calm about everything, and maybe that's why. When you go through something like that, you learn how to put things into perspective.

For us, it was very painful. But it was also a miracle in our family's eyes. It could have been a horrendous thing we would never get over, but we did.

It was quite a while for me before I was able to sit there and watch the news reports of my father's accident. I talked to Roger about three years afterward; we met in Colorado to go skiing. It was the first time I was able to sit down and talk with him about events from his point of view, how the events played out.

In the beginning, we weren't concerned about *how* things happened; we were just concerned about, "Did they find him? Is he okay?" And "How are his feet? And hands?"

It was hard for me to hear it. I read the draft of the book, and it was hard. I didn't think it would be hard for me, but it was hard—going back and thinking about everything again.

It was a very traumatic experience that turned out for the best.

APPENDIX TWO

RULES

Nick Williams' Five Golden Rules for Survival and Success

- One: Persevere

- Two: Use Teamwork

- Three: Be Resourceful

- Four: Be Committed

- Five: Keep a Positive Attitude

Check out these other fine titles by Durban House
online or at your local book store.

EXCEPTIONAL BOOKS
BY
EXCEPTIONAL WRITERS

NONFICTION

FISH HEADS, RICE, RICE WINE & WAR: A VIETNAM PARADOX	Lt. Col. Thomas G. Smith, Ret.
JIMMY CARTER AND THE RISE OF MILITANT ISLAM	Philip Pilevsky
MIDDLE ESSENCE— WOMEN OF WONDER YEARS	Landy Reed
SPORES, PLAGUES, AND HISTORY: THE STORY OF ANTHRAX	Chris Holmes
WHITE WITCH DOCTOR	Dr. John A. Hunt
PROTOCOL	Mary Jane McCaffree, Pauline Innis, and Richard Sand.

For 25 years, the bible for public relations firms, corporations, embassies, foreign governments, and individuals seeking to do business with the Federal Government.

DURBAN HOUSE FICTION

A DREAM ACROSS TIME   Annie Rogers

Jamie Elliott arrives from New York onto the lush Caribbean island of St. Lucia, and finds herself caught up in Island forces, powerful across the centuries, which find deep echoes in her recurring dreams.

AFTER LIFE LIFE   Don Goldman

A hilarious murder mystery taking place in the afterlife. Andrew Law, Chief Justice of the Texas Supreme Court, is the Picture of robust health when he suddenly dies. Upon arriving in The afterlife, Andy discovers he was murdered, and his untimely has some unexpected, and far-reaching consequences—a worldwide depression, among others. Many diabolical plots are woven in this funny, fast-paced whodunit, with a surprising double-cross ending.

an-eye-for-an-eye.com   Dennis Powell

Jed Warren, Vietnam Peacenik, and Jeff Porter, ex-Airborne, were close friends and executives at Megafirst Bank. So when CEO McAlister crashes the company, creams off millions in bonuses, and wipes out Jed and Jeff, things began to happen.

If you wonder about corporate greed recorded in today's newspapers, read what one man did about it in this intricate, devious, and surprise-ending thriller.

BASHA   John Hamilton Lewis

LA reviewer, Jeff Krieder's pick as "Easily my best read of the year." Set in the world of elite professional tennis, and rooted in ancient Middle East hatreds of identity and blood loyalties, Basha is charged with the fiercely competitive nature of professional sports, and the dangers of terrorism. An already simmering Middle East begins to boil, and CIA Station Chief Grant Corbet must track down the highly successful terrorist, Basha, In a deadly race against time Grant hunts the illusive killer only to see his worst nightmare realized.

THE CORMORANT DOCUMENTS   Robert Middlemiss

Who is Cormorant, and why is his coded letter on Hitler's stationary found on a WWII Nazi bomber preserved in the Arctic? And why is the plane loaded with Goering's plundered are treasures? Mallory must find out or die. On the run from the British Secret Service and CIA, he finds himself caught in a secret that dates back to 1945.

CRISIS PENDING   Stephen Cornell

When U.S. oil refineries blow up, the White House and the Feds move fast, but not fast enough. Sherman Nassar Ramsey, terrorist for hire, a loner, brilliant, multilingual, and skilled with knives, pistols, and bare hands, moves around the country with contempt, ease and cunning.

As America's fuel system starts grinding to a halt, rioting breaks out for gasoline, and food becomes scarce, events draw Lee Hamilton's wife, Mary, into the crisis. And when Ramsey kidnaps her, the battle becomes very personal.

DANGER WITHIN   Mark Danielson

Over 100 feet down in cold ocean waters lies the wreck of pilot Kevin Hamilton's DC-10. In it are secrets which someone is desperate to keep. When the Navy sends a team of divers from the Explosives Ordinance Division, a mysterious explosion from the wreck almost destroys the salvage ship. The FBI steps in with Special Agent Mike Pentaglia. Track the life and death of Global Express Flight 3217 inside the gritty world of aviation, and discover the shocking cargo that was hidden on its last flight.

DEADLY ILLUMINATION   Serena Stier

It's summer 1890 in New York City. A ebullient young woman, Florence Tod, must challenge financier, John Pierpont Morgan, to solve a possible murder. J.P.'s librarian has ingested poison embedded in an illumination of a unique Hildegard van Bingen manuscript. Florence and her cousin, Isabella Stewart Gardner, discover the corpse. When Isabella secretly removes a gold tablet from the scene of the crime, she sets off a chain of events that will involve Florence and her in a dangerous conspiracy.

HANDS OF VENGEANCE   Richard Sand

Private detective Lucas Rook returns still haunted by the murder of his twin brother. What seems like an easy case involving workplace violations, the former homicide detective finds himself locked in a life and death struggle with the deadly domestic terrorist group, The Brothers of the Half Moon. A must-read for lovers of dark mysteries.

HOUR OF THE WOLVES   Stephane Daimlen-
                                              Völs

After more than three centuries, the *Poisons Affair* remains one of history's great, unsolved mysteries. The worst impulses of human nature—sordid sexual perversion, murderous intrigues, witchcraft, Satanic cults—thrive within the shadows of the Sun King's absolutism and will culminate in the darkest secret of his reign; the infamous *Poisons Affair*, a remarkably complex web of horror, masked by Baroque splendor, luxury and refinement.

A HOUSTON WEEKEND   Orville Palmer

Professor Edward Randall, not-yet-forty, divorced and separated from his daughters, is leading a solitary, cheerless existence in a university town. At a conference in Houston, he runs into his childhood sweetheart. Then she was poverty-stricken, American Indian. Now she's elegantly attired, driving an expensive Italian car and lives in a millionaires' enclave. Will their fortuitous encounter grow into anything meaningful?

JOHNNIE RAY AND MISS KILGALLEN   Bonnie Hearn Hill
                                              and Larry Hill

Based on the real-life love affair between 1950's singer Johnnie Ray and columnist Dorothy Kilgallen. They had everything—wealth, fame, celebrity. The last thing they needed was love. *Johnnie Ray and Miss Kilgallen* is a love story that travels at a dangerous, roaring speed. Driven close to death from their excesses, both try to regain their lives and careers in a novel that goes beyond the bounds of mere biography.

THE LATERAL LINE   Robert Middlemiss

Kelly Travert was ready. She had the Israeli assassination pistol, she had coated the bullets with garlic, and tonight she would kill the woman agent who tortured and killed her father. When a negotiator for the CIA warns her, suddenly her father's death is not so simple anymore.

LEGACY OF A STAR   Peter Longley

Greed and murder run rampant—the prize: desert commerce of untold wealth, and the saving of the Jews. From the high temples to Roman barracks; from bat filled caves to magnificent villas on a sun-drenched sea; to the chamber of Salome, and the barren brothels where Esther rules, the Star moves across the heavens and men die—while a child is born.

LETHAL CURE   Kurt Popke

Dr. Jake Prescott is a resident on duty in the emergency room when medics rush in with a double trauma involving patients sustaining injuries during a home invasion. Jake learns that one patient is the intruder, the other, his wife, Sara. He also learns that his four-year-old daughter, Kelly, is missing, and his patient may hold the key to her recovery.

THE MEDUSA STRAIN   Chris Holmes

Finalist for *ForeWord Magazine's* 'Book of the Year'. A gripping tale of bio-terrorism that stunningly portrays the dangers of chemical warfare. Mohammed Ali Ossman, a bitter Iraqi scientist who hates America, breeds a deadly form of anthrax, and develops a diabolical means to initiate an epidemic. It is a story of personal courage in the face of terror, and of lost love found.

MR. IRRELEVANT   Jerry Marshall

Booklist Star Review. Chesty Hake, the last man chosen in the NFL draft, has been dubbed Mr. Irrelevant. By every yardstick, he should not be playing pro football, but because of his heart and high threshold for pain, he endures. Then during his eighth and final season, he slides into paranoia, and football will never be the same.

OPAL EYE DEVIL   John Hamilton Lewis

"Best historical thriller in decades." *Good Books*. In the age of the Robber Baron, *Opal Eye Devil* weaves an extraordinary tale about the brave men and women who risk everything as the discovery of oil rocks the world. The richness and pageantry of two great cultures, Great Britain and China, are brought together in a thrilling tale of adventure and human relationships.

PRIVATE JUSTICE   Richard Sand

Ben Franklin Award 'Best Mystery of the Year'. After taking brutal revenge for the murder of his twin brother, Lucas Rooks leaves the NYPD to become a private eye. A father turns to Rook to investigate the murder of his daughter. Rook's dark journey finds him racing to find the killer, who kills again and again as *Private Justice* careens toward a startling end.

ROADHOUSE BLUES   Baron R. Birtcher

From the sun-drenched sands of Santa Catalina Island to the smoky night clubs and back alleys of West Hollywood, Roadhouse Blues is a taut noir thriller. Newly retired Homicide detective Mike Travis is torn from the comfort of his chartered yacht business into the dark, bizarre underbelly of Los Angeles's music scene by a grisly string of murders.

RUBY TUESDAY   Baron R. Birtcher

When Mike Travis sails into the tropical harbor of Kona, Hawaii, he expects to put LA Homicide behind him. Instead, he finds the sometimes seamy back streets and dark underbelly of a tropical paradise and the world of music and high finance, where wealth and greed are steeped in sex, vengeance, and murder.

SAMSARA   John Hamilton Lewis

A thrilling tale of love and violence set in post-World War II Hong Kong. Nick Ridley, a captain in the RAF, is captured and sent to the infamous Japanese prisoner-of-war camp, Changi, in Singapore. He survives brutal treatment at the hands of the camp commandant, Colonel Tetsuro Matashima. Nick moves to Hong Kong, where he reunites with the love of his life, Courtney, and builds a world-class airline. On the eve of having his company recognized at the Crown Colony's official carrier, Courtney is kidnapped, and people begin to die. Nick is pulled into the quagmire, and must once again face the demon of Changi.

SECRET OF THE SCROLL   Chester D. Campbell

Finalist '*Deadly Dagger*' award, and *ForeWord Magazine's* 'Book of the Year' award. Deadly groups of Palestinians and Israelis struggle to gain possession of an ancient parchment that was unknowingly smuggled from Israel to the U.S. by a retired Air Force investigator. Col. Greg McKenzie finds himself mired in the duplicitous world of Middle East politics when his wife is taken hostage in an effort to force the return of the first-century Hebrew scroll.

SECRETS ARE ANONYMOUS   Frederick L. Cullen

A comic mystery with a cast of characters who weave multiple plots, puzzles, twists, and turns. A remarkable series of events unfold in the lives of a dozen residents of Bexley, Ohio. The journalism career of the principle character is derailed when her father shows up for her college graduation with his boyfriend on his way to a new life in California.

THE SEESAW SYNDROME   Michael Madden

A terrifying medical thriller that slices with a scalpel, exposing the greed and corruption that can happen when drug executives and medical researchers position themselves for huge profits. Biosense Pharmaceeuticals has produced a drug named Floragen, and now they need to test it on patients to gain FDA approval. But there's a problem with the new drug. One of the side effects included death.

THE SERIAL KILLER'S DIET BOOK   Kevin Postupack

Finalist *ForeWord Magazine's* Book of the Year' award. Fred Orbis is fat, but he dreams of being Frederico Orbisini, internationally known novelist, existential philosopher, raconteur, and lover of women. Both a satire and a reflection on morals, God and the Devil, beauty, literature, and the best-seller-list, *The Serial Killer's Diet Book* is a delightful look at the universal human longing to become someone else.

THE STREET OF FOUR WINDS   Andrew Lazarus

Paris, just after World War II. A time for love, but also a time of political ferment. In the Left Bank section of the city, Tom Cortell, a tough, intellectual journalist, finally learns the meaning of love. Along with him is a gallery of fascinating characters who lead a merry and sometimes desperate chase between Paris, Switzerland, and Spain in search of themselves.

TUNNEL RUNNER   Richard Sand

A fast, deadly espionage thriller peopled with quirky and sometimes vicious characters, *Tunnel Runner* tells of a dark world where murder is committed and no one is brought to account, where loyalties exist side by side with lies and extreme violence.

WHAT GOES AROUND   Don Goldman
    Finalist *ForeWord Magazine's* 'Book of the Year' award. Ray Banno, a medical researcher, was wrongfully incarcerated for bank fraud. *What Goes Around* is a dazzling tale of deception, treachery, revenge, and nonstop action that resolves around money, sex, and power. The book's sharp insight and hard-hitting style builds a high level of suspense as Banno strives for redemption.

DURBAN HOUSE NONFICTION

FISH HEADS, RICE, RICE WINE & WAR   LTC. Thomas G.
Smith (Ret.)
    A human, yet humorous, look at the strangest and most misunderstood war ever, in which American soldiers were committed. Readers are offered an insiders view of American life in the midst of highly deplorable conditions, which often lead to laughter.

JIMMY CARTER AND THE RISE   Philip Pilevsky
OF MILITANT ISLAM
    One of America's foremost authorities on the Middle East, Philip Pilevsky argues that President Jimmy Carter's failure to support the Shah of Iran led to the 1979 revolution. That revolution legitimized and provided a base of operations for militant Islamists across the Middle East. A most thought provoking book.

MIDDLE ESSENCE...   Landy Reed
WOMEN OF WONDER YEARS
    A wonderful book by renowned speaker, Landy Reed that shows how real women in real circumstances have confronted and conquered the obstacles of midlife. This is a must have guide and companion to what can be the most significant and richest years of a woman's life.

PROTOCOL   Mary Jane McCaffree,
(25th Anniversary Edition)   Pauline Innis, and
                                        Richard Sand
    Protocol is a comprehensive guide to proper diplomatic, official and social usage. The Bible for foreign governments, embassies, corporations, public relations firms, and individuals wishing to do business with the Federal Government. "A wealth of detail on every conceivable question, from titles and forms of address to ceremonies and flag etiquette." Department of State Newsletter.

SPORES, PLAGUES, HISTORY: Chris Holmes
THE STORY OF ANTHRAX

"Much more than the story of a microbe. It is the tale of history and proph-
ecy woven into a fabric of what was, what might have been and what might yet
be. What you are about to read is real—your are not in the Twilight Zone—
adjusting your TV set will not change the picture. However, it is not hopeless,
and we are not helpless. The same technology used to create biological weapons
can protect us with better vaccines and treatments." CDR Ted J. Robinson, *U.S.
Navy Epidemiologist.*

WHITE WITCH DOCTOR   John A. Hunt

A true story of life and death, hope and despair in apartheid-ruled South
Africa. White Witch Doctor details, white surgeon, John Hunt's fight to save his
beloved country in a time of social unrest and political upheaval, drawing readers
into the world of South African culture, mores and folkways, superstitions, and
race relations.